The Hungarian Connection

The Roots of Photojournalism

László Beke
Gábor Szilágyi
Klára Tőry

Edited by Colin Ford

1987

NATIONAL MUSEUM OF PHOTOGRAPHY FILM AND TELEVISION
Prince's View BRADFORD BD5 OTR West Yorkshire
The National Museum of Photography, Film & Television is part of the Science Museum, London

Cover: János Müllner: *Fish-Seller*, 1910s

Back Cover: Károly Escher: *Does the Man Always go First?* 1934

Designed by Imelda Kay NMPFT Design Office
Printed by Jackson Wilson Ltd, Leeds

ISBN No. 0-948489-06-5

Photographs reproduced by permission of

The Museum of the Hungarian Working Class Movement
The Association of Hungarian Photo Artists
The Hungarian Historical Museum
The National Library
The National Museum of Fine Arts

Without the willingness of these Budapest institutions to lend us their precious originals, there could have been no exhibition and no book. As Keeper of the National Museum of Photography, Film and Television, I wish to express my sincere gratitude to them and to their ever-helpful staffs.

The exhibition was brought together in Budapest by the Műcsarnok Art Gallery. We at the Museum owe our thanks to its Director, Katalin Néray, and to Marianna Mayer.

As editor of this booklet, I thank and congratulate the three Hungarian authors (and their translators) who have risen so ably and so articulately to the challenge of conveying to us who know so little the photographic history and characteristics of their country.

Above all, I would like to express my personal and heartfelt gratitude to Gabor Horvath (Cultural Attaché of the Hungarian People's Republic in London) and Peter Korniss (photographer and editor *extraordinaire*). They have consistently encouraged and supported The Hungarian Connection at every step. I am proud to acknowledge their unstinting help and warm friendship.

C. F.

The Hungarian Connection

For me, the search for the 'Hungarian Connection' began in October 1979. Commissioned by the Arts Council of Great Britain to write the catalogue for a retrospective exhibition of photographs by André Kertész, I spent two days in New York interviewing the then 85 years' old master. As we talked, I realised that the roots of his pioneering and influential style lay deep in his native land (which he had left in 1925). If Kertész's art owed so much to his Hungarian origins, was not the same probably true of the impressive number of Hungarian emigré photographers who had so shaped the history of the medium – and especially photojournalism – in the twentieth century?

The names of some of those influential Hungarians are cited early in the first essay in this book, *Just Suppose. . .* by the teacher, historian and art critic László Beke. His contribution, too modestly sub-titled 'Some Notes on an Outline History of Hungarian Photography', provides a context in which to understand the history, and how it led to a whole generation of early photojournalists.

For Hungary, the end of the First World War signalled the collapse of a monarchy, the loss of authority over many ethnic groups and a dramatic reduction in her territory. The Petit Trianon Treaty (4 June 1920) gave some two-thirds of the area of the nation to her neighbours: Romania, Yugoslavia, Czechoslovakia. Tens of thousands of Hungarians, finding themselves residents of 'foreign countries', hastily moved into what was left of Hungary. There was overcrowding, poverty, and considerable political unrest, but also a considerable enrichening of the cultural climate. Artists of all kinds and from different backgrounds were thrown together. There was an explosion in almost all the arts including photography.

The new artistic climate spawned many illustrated magazines, published in Budapest and other Hungarian cities. Full of engravings and, sometimes, photographs, they provided a visual education for many: Kertész has testified to the influence of such magazines, and to the fact that at the age of six he hoped to be able to make such pictures one day. The photographer for one of the magazines (*Pesti Naplo*), Márton Munkácsi, claimed to be the highest paid in the country (later, he made the same claim about his earnings in the USA).

When, in 1986, thanks to generous support from the Embassy of the Hungarian People's Republic and the British Council's Visiting Arts Unit, I went to Budapest to do some detective work, I began with those illustrated magazines. In particular, Kertész had told me that two of his earliest pictures, taken while he was in the Army during the First World War, had won small prizes in a competition for soldiers' photographs in the weekly *Érdekes Úsjág* ('Interesting Happenings'). In Budapest's National Library, I found that the competition had run almost throughout the war, and that hundreds of photographs (mostly by amateurs) had been published. A generous selection were later re-printed in large gravure portfolios, and it is these which form the basis of the first section of *The Hungarian Connection* exhibition. When I met the historian and critic Gábor Szilágyi, I found he was as excited by the *Érdekes Úsjág* War Albums as I – and vastly more knowledgeable. I am most grateful to him for sharing his knowledge with us in his informative essay.

Beyond the National Library, I began to look at other museum collections. At first, of course, the photographers' names meant little to me, but gradually one above all began to emerge as surely a master to rank with the most famous: János Müllner. It transpired that, even in Hungary, Müllner is a shadowy figure, so I am once again grateful to Gábor Szilágyi for so usefully assembling the facts.

The most succinct description of the characteristics of Kertész's photographs is his own: 'little happenings'. He was always interested in the everyday life of ordinary people, which he captured as it were in sidelong glances. Sixty or seventy years ago, many Hungarian photographers shared the same concerns and, if their results were rarely as good as Kertész's (we should not expect to discover a lot more geniuses!) they certainly show that his interests were by no means unique. This section of the exhibition shows as clearly as any why so many photojournalists sprang from such a background. Its selection owes a good deal to the perceptive eye of the contemporary Hungarian photographer, Peter Korniss, who continued to search for 'little happenings' after my return to England.

The last section of the exhibition and booklet is devoted to Károly Escher. Escher is 'the one who stayed behind', a photographer whose range, authority and sheer longevity undoubtedly earn him a place in the worldwide story of photography. Fortunately, a considerable number of his original exhibition prints are preserved in the important collection of The Association of Hungarian Photo Artists. Consistently encouraging my research, and apparently welcoming this outsider's view, the Association agreed to lend these prints, and made them freely available to Klára Tőry, who was thus able to write a perceptive essay about Escher.

My debt to those named, and the lenders acknowledged on Page 2 is apparent. Without them, there could have been no exhibition, no book, and no 'Hungarian Connection'. I hope they will now share my view that, for one period at least, Hungary was in the forefront of world photography.

Among many reasons for this pre-eminence, one which does not emerge from research or display can only come from personal knowledge. At the beginning of my search, I asked the distinguished Hungarian emigré publisher, Andor Kraszna-Krausz (founder of Britain's Focal Press), just why there were so many photographers in and around Budapest all those years ago. He remembered being given a cheap box camera for his eleventh or twelfth birthday and that this was very common. It may seem a trivial fact, but it shows that photography really was part of many people's lives – even children (Károly Escher, too, took up photography at the age of twelve). That has never been true in Britain, nor is it even today, when there are so many foolproof and automatic cameras.

The moral, for any nation, seems obvious: start them young, show them lots of pictures, and perhaps you will produce another generation of great photographers!

Colin Ford
Keeper
National Museum of Photography,
Film & Television

Just Suppose. . .

Some Notes on an Outline History of Hungarian Photography

Sooner or later, every country comes to write its own history of photography – and finds it virtually the same as everywhere else. All over the world, people tried to capture and secure images at about the same time. Always there were arguments – but different types of photography, some relatively dependable, others not, seem to have reached every country with, at most, a couple of years between them. Only the people, the objects and the scenery were different.

At least, that's how it was until the appearance of the first conscious photo-artists. But who can adequately decide which photograph is artistic and which is not? Especially in the nineteenth century, when the only difference between two portraits might be that the sitter in one looks more handsome than the other? Or today, when technically mediocre amateur works may have as much feeble charm as the carefully-considered compositions of any 'photo-artist'.

Granted all this, who could unequivocally tell the true history of Hungarian art-photography? Even our most reliable stereotypes betray us. If we think of the many famous photo-artists we gave to the world – Lászlo Moholy-Nagy, Márton Munkácsi, Robert Capa, Brassaï, André Kertész, etc – we realise that they all reached world fame in foreign lands, with foreign equipment and materials, with foreign themes and foreign ways of thinking!

This curious fact is worth pondering. Just suppose. . . what would have happened if these world celebrities had not emigrated after the First World War? Perhaps they would not have become photograhers at all. Or maybe they would be second-rate photographers in small, dusty provincial towns. Perhaps, alternately, their photojournalism, rather than the pseudo-folkloric 'Hungarian' style, would have become world-famous between the two wars. We could have become a photo-superpower. . .

Just suppose it had not been Daguerre, but Farkas Bólyai who first discovered photography? There are many signs that seem to indicate that this embittered teacher from Transylvania, a polymath who never quite succeeded in anything, had found some kind of process to secure images at least a decade before the daguerrotype was announced publicly. Nothing came of it.

Just suppose the Austrian Emperor Ferdinand V had reacted more positively on examining the daguerreotype which Daguerre sent to him in spring 1839, as well as to Chancellor Metternich and to his ambassador in Paris, Count Antal Apponvi (the latter can be seen today in the collection of the National Technical Museum). Suppose he had, say, purchased the patent rights?

Just suppose it had been József Petzval, the inventor in 1840 of the high-speed portrait lens, who gave his name to so many famous cameras, rather than Voigtlander, who as an entrepreneur and manufacturer only supplied the tubes for them? Just suppose that the distinguished art historian and archaeologist of old Hungary, Imre Henszlmann, had not, in his 1841 essay *Parallel Between Classic and Modern Artistic Ideas and Teachings, with Special Regard to Artistic Development in Hungary*, taken a stand entirely opposed to the artistic nature of photography?

And today? Just suppose, to take an example, that after so many decades a museum of the history of photography were finally established in Hungary, as advanced photographic training has already begun at the Budapest College of Design and Industrial Arts? Suppose it not only propagated technical knowledge, but a modern attitude as well? Suppose it trained not only practising photographers, but photo-historians and theoreticians – so that more than the current handful of experts could examine this immense field.

These things did not happen. But posing the question 'Just suppose. . .' emphasises that the history of photography as a technical medium is more or less the same throughout the world. But photography as an art, though only a segment in the whole of photography, is much more varied and subjective. If we want to show the world a specifically Hungarian photographic art, we must bring to light all that develops only here, and we should concentrate resolutely on works which could originate nowhere else in the world.

Only thus can one avoid the history of Hungarian art-photography being no more than a compound of accidents and subjective improvisations. This is what the 'just suppose. . .?' question ultimately leads to.

From the conditional to the affirmative. The newspaper-reading public in Hungary did indeed learn of Daguerre's invention as early as 2 February 1839, from the pages of *Hasznosm Mulatságok* ('Useful Experiments'). Daguerrotypes were made in early 1840 or before, if not in Pest or Buda, then in Zagreb. In the spring of that year, Daguerre's book appeared in translation. In June 1841, Jacopo Marastoni, a painter of Venetian birth, opened the first photographic studio in Pest (we know one daguerreotype by him, in reproduction).

By the mid 1850s, tens of thousands of daguerreotypes had probably been made around the country though, at the time of the 1979 History of Photography exhibition, we could identify scarcely 200. Today, the number has grown to almost 400, counting those which survive only in reproduction. They are almost exclusively portraits or group pictures, taken by professionals working to commission (in Transylvania, there was an ambitious group of amateur experimenters, led by Miklós Zevk, but we know relatively little of their work).

A daguerrotype of the Virgin Mary church in Buda is an exception, as is the superb series in which Ádám Gola preserved István Ferenczy's sculpture of designs for the King Mathias memorial before their destruction in 1846. Talbot's process, the calotype, was less widespread than the daguerreotype, so such rarities as the negatives and prints prepared for colouring from the studio of József Skopáll in Győr are especially important. A Hungarian photographer, János Tiedge, was awarded a prize at the 1862 London Exhibition for his traditional costume pictures; they were probably taken on glass negatives.

The "heroic age of photography" began in the 1850's. As the wet plate or collodion process appeared, so did the experimenters, with their immense, portable cameras and laboratories. Antal Simonyi won an award at the 1855 Paris Exhibition with some kind of instantaneous photography process and, on his way home, inspired by the ideas of utopian socialism, enthusiastically wrote of the new social possibilities of industrial-tehnical development. From 1854 onwards, Ferenc Veress operated in Kolozsvár; later, he experimented for decades with colour photography, and charted the landscapes and memorials of Transylvania. His initiatives were further developed into a systematic scientific undertaking by Balázs Orbán, who took photographs for volumes of *A Description of the Szekely Region (1868-73).* Though only engravings could be reproduced in the book, a substantial number of these original photographs survive. Károly Szathmáry Pap took photographs of the Crimean War; Pal Rosti visited Mexico and Cuba in 1857-58 and was perhaps the world's first to compile photo-albums of these parts of Latin-America.

The two most influential photographers of the second part of the century, Károly Divald and György Klősz, began their careers in the 1860s. Divald opened a studio in Eperjes in 1863 and went on to photograph the whole of upper Northern Hungary. Klősz set up a studio in Budapest in 1896. It is his pictures which document the 1896 Millennial festivities, and which give us the most comprehensive portrayal of city life.

In Hungary as elsewhere in the world, the relationship between photography and art was always an subject of debate. Photography was first formally accepted as one of the 'liberal arts' in 1872, but the decision had the drawback that all sorts of people now felt they could be photographers. Painters who were no longer getting commissions, for instance. In the early 1860s the most famous were Miklos Barabas and József Borsos. In 1863, Bertalan Székely, a sort of Hungarian Delacroix, spoke up against photography on theoretical grounds but he too had probably used it as an aid to painting. At the end of the decade, Mihály Munkácsy made exceptional preparatory photographs for some of his major compositions, such as 'Condemned Cell,' and 'Linden Shredders'.

By the 1870s, Hungary was flooded with *cartes de visite,* retouched, with studio backgrounds and props, often hand-coloured. Sometimes a famous person or an interesting oddity stands out from the mass. There are technical curiosities, like Sándor Strelinsky's gigantic composite tableau *The Csardas* – a lively Hungarian national dance (1895), or Mihály Esterházy's instantaneous photograph of a high-jumper (1885); or Jenő Gothard's or Miklós Konkoly Thege's astronomical photographs, or the high-altitude pictures by the world famous physicist and passionate mountain climber, Lorand Eotoves (eg *Night in the Dolomites*).

In this sense, everything by the great Hungarian travellers, geographers or ethnographers – Ferenc Hopp, Ármin Vámbéry, Lajos Lóczy the elder, Jenő Zichy, Lajos Biró, Mór Dechy, János Xantus, Samu Teleki, etc – is interesting. The field is almost unexplored, though it would be of great interest, not only for the history of Hungarian photography. These early pictures should be taken back to their places of origin – Africa, Siberia, Central Asia, Indonesia or China – to be placed beside the photographs taken there by other nationalities. From such a direct comparison, our travellers might earn a proper place in photo history.

Most of these photographers were amateurs. It was an amateur, Vince Wartha, who founded the Circle of the Friends of Photography in 1894. Gradually, commercial and art photography were growing apart. According to some estimates, there were by 1880 some 250-300 professional photographers in Hungary, but only 30-40 amateurs; the proportions were to reverse. The Budapest Photo Club was founded in 1899; the National Association of Hungarian Amateurs in 1905.

Meanwhile, photography continued to imitate painting – in landscapes, portraits, still lifes, etc – in soft-tone and platinotype, rubber and bromoil prints by István Kerny, Jacques Faix, the two remarkable women portraitists Olga Máté and Ilka Révai, and two photographers who were our first film cameramen, Dénes Ronai and György Haranghy. Haranghy's first film *The Land of Mirages* was presented in 1902 in Budapest. The film inspired the great Hungarian visionary painter, Tivadar Kosztka Csontvary, to create his famous 'Hortobágy'. It was not only amateurs who imitated painting, but the most important professionals, foremost among them Aladár Székely, who invested the artists, authors and intellectuals in his turn of the century portraits with a kind of 'psychological realism' (see, for example, his famous Endre Ady series!). Or the young József Pécsi, creator of portraits of Nijinsky and Pavlova, who depicts himself and the painter Lajos Gulácsy in Renaissance costume and setting. Pécsi succeeded Székely as the prototype professional photographer of outstanding taste and culture, whose studio is a kind of social and literary salon, always keeping abreast of the latest tendencies in photography.

Alongside these metropolitan photo-artists we find such simple provincials as József Plohn from Hódmezővásárhely, who documented the ethnography of his region, helped the painter János Tornyay design strikingly sombre genre paintings, and made a totally un-pictorial series of photographs of veterans of the Hungarian War of Independence (1848/9).

The number of photographs made in the First World War is immense and their place in photographic history largely unexplored. It was the time of the birth of modern press photography. Márton Munkácsi and André Kertész both began their careers, the latter leaving a substantial reportage from his early life in Hungary. Bela Révész and Lájos Biró also started as reporters; like the outstandingly gifted János Müllner, they followed the events of the 1919 Commune.

After the First World War, Hungarian photography split into two rigidly opposed camps: on the one hand were a few committed Left wing documentarists, on the other a far larger number of conservative amateurs who idealised and softened their subject matter in the so-called 'Magyar' (Hungarian) style. Though this seems typically Hungarian, the true essence of the age lay in extreme diversity, and even in the combination of different aesthetics and ideologies. But the Magyar style became dominant, practised by professionals (Rudolf Balogh) and amateurs (Ervin Dulovits, Ernő Vadas) alike. Magyar landscape, Magyar puszta (plains), Magyar villages, Magyar costume: it all seemed aimed at tourists, its glamour highlighted by painterly processes and soft focus lenses.

This romanticism had an urban equivalent in the dreamy nudes, child studies and city-scapes of such photographers as Dénes Rónai and Pál Angelo. Late in the 1920s, a few artists turned cautiously towards 'Neue Sachlichkeit' (New Objectivity): Nándor Bárány, Tibor Hegyei, Tibor Csörgeő, Kálman Szöllősy, Zoltán Zajky.

If we look for the ideology of the Left, we find only some critical studies of village life, among them the astonishing 'Tiborc' series by Kata Kálmán. There are some genuine press photographers who took pictures of practically everything professionally, but whose greatest achievements were done in their 'own time' (Sándor Bojár, Károly Escher). It is worth noting how photography of the Left offered chances to women: Kata Sugár, Klára Langer and Teréz Bergmann are perhaps the most important examples.

From 1928 on, the most determinedly Left wing photographers gathered round Lajos Kassák's periodical *Munka* ('Work'). Their open criticism of society led to direct police action on the occasion of the exhibition *Our Life* (1932). The show was closed and its two organisers arrested. The *Munka* style combined classical documentary methods with photomontage and 'New Objectivity'.

After the Second World War (and particularly after 1949/50), photography developed in a strangely paradoxical way. The new Hungary wanted to shape its photographic style by adding socialist realism to the best traditions of documentary, and a photo-artists' section was started in The Association of Hungarian Artists and Designers in order to bring this about. But, without realising it, they reverted to the old 'arty' pre-war techniques.

Though things did not improve much with the formation of the Association of Hungarian Photo Artists in 1956, a new generation appeared in the mid 1960's. György Lőrinczy, Csaba Koncz and others experimented with micro-realism, abstraction and subjective photography while the documentarists, aiming at a direct portrayal of society, found a new strength alongside film-makers who had similar ambitions. The main problem with this movement is that, because the best documentary photography adopts a critical stance, it found itself turning more and more to the fringes of society when it should properly have been tackling more central issues.

At the end of the sixties, as elsewhere in the world, fine art started to move in on photography, in the work of András Baranyay, Dóra Maurer and a dozen or so others. This has affected the attitude of the younger generation, and today we see a refined mixture of fine art techniques (János Vető) alongside classically plain (Gábor Kerekes) or 'post New Wave' straight photography (Lenke Szilágyi). It is virtually the same story as everywhere else in the world. Just suppose, though, that it had been different. . .?

Lászlo Beke
(Translated by András Szántó)

An Album of War

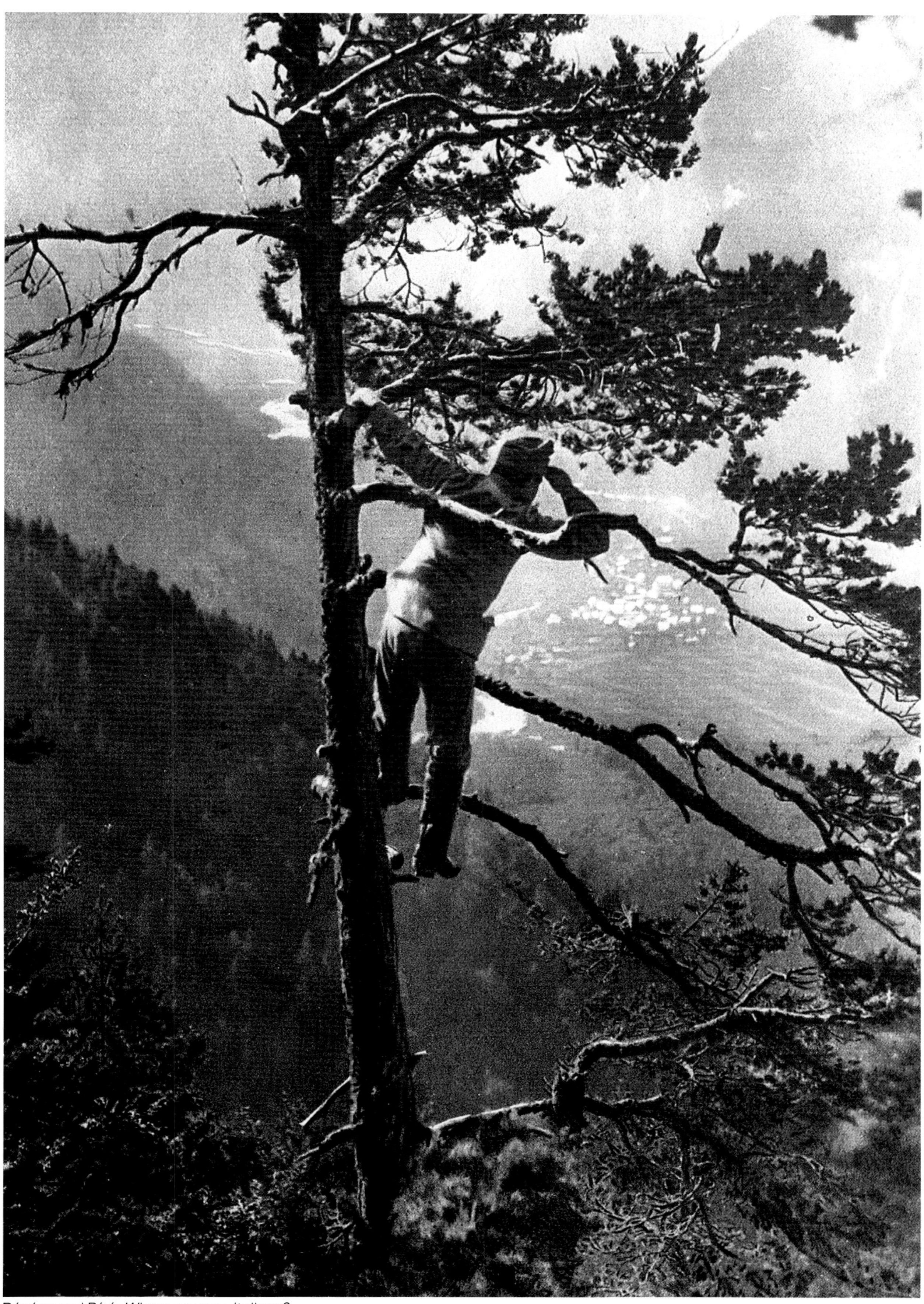

Révész and Bíró: *Where are you, Italians?*

The Competition

When the new daily *Érdekes Úsjág* ('Interesting Happenings') first appeared, on 23 March 1913, it was the only Hungarian newspaper able to boast of 'having secured the patent to reproduce pictures by rotogravure'. Fully aware of this advantage over its competitors, it seized every opportunity to publish as many photographs as possible.

Little more than a year later came what was perhaps the biggest opportunity ever for photographic journalism: the First World War. Six months after the outbreak of hostilities, *Érdekes Úsjág* launched its photographic competition for serving soldiers. Entries, which had to be unpublished, were expected to depict the war activities of the Hungarian Monarchy:

> *'We believe and hope that our competition will encourage those soldiers who have spent the rare moments of rest on the front to take pictures and have enriched the war issues of Érdekes Úsjág'.*

The first prize of a generous 3000 crowns helped attract a grand total of 1599 entries, many more than expected, and the fact that scarcely a Hungarian family was not affected by the war made the competition popular with readers. So sensational was the magazine's war coverage that editors in Austria, Germany, Holland and Spain requested pictures for publication. *Érdekes Úsjág*, delighted with its success, announced a second competition:

> *'The glorious achievements of the Hungarian army have so far been communicated to the neutral nations only in words, but now these pictures will tell the world at large about Hungarian triumphs on the battlefield; the bravery, dedication and resolution of Hungarian soldiers; and the endurance and perseverance of the nation at home'.*

The second competition had the same top prize as before but more specific conditions. This time, entries were expected both to 'reflect the life and battle of our glorious army, which has deeply penetrated enemy territory' and to 'give witness to our soldiers' invincible spirit, wonderful pride and human qualities, and to the good aspects of war, whose real heroes are parents, mothers and wives'.

This time, 1400 entries were received, and on 1 September 1916 a third competition was launched, with the hope that some entries would 'have no other *raison d'être* but beauty and finesse'. A month later, the editors announced the awards, and their belief that they now had 'the most beautiful and interesting' archive of the war and its progress, together with a record of its effects on soldiers and citizens. The photographs, 'showing the horrid yet majestic nature of war' showed activities behind the battle-lines and provided 'evidence of the good humour and character of Hungarian soldiers'. Furthermore, they were a real encouragement to amateur photographers.

After all this, a fourth 3000 crown prize competition was inevitable. Its only condition was that the subject-matter of photographs must be Hungarian and it attracted a record 1796 entries. But there semed a real danger that the whole exercise might disintegrate into pointlessness, and entries for the fifth competition were therefore required to be topical and news-worthy rather than merely 'artistic'.

The Albums

When the first competition finished, *Érdekes Úsjág* published an album of its 'exceptionally rich material'. The ten parts each contained twelve 19cm x 36cm rotogravure pictures, wrapped in dark grey elegantly lettered cardboard folders. Readers were promised their money back if they were dissatisfied and were assured that:

> *'These pictures from the battlefield, whether they are bound in a fancy cover and lie in the living-rooms of Hungarian families, or are framed . . . will always be good memories . . . of the unforgettable days whose exciting atmosphere we are living through'.*

After the second competition, the newspaper announced another album, 'to include the rare and the beautiful as well as outstanding events and an artistic rendering of war'. The third competition 'greatly extended and perfected this

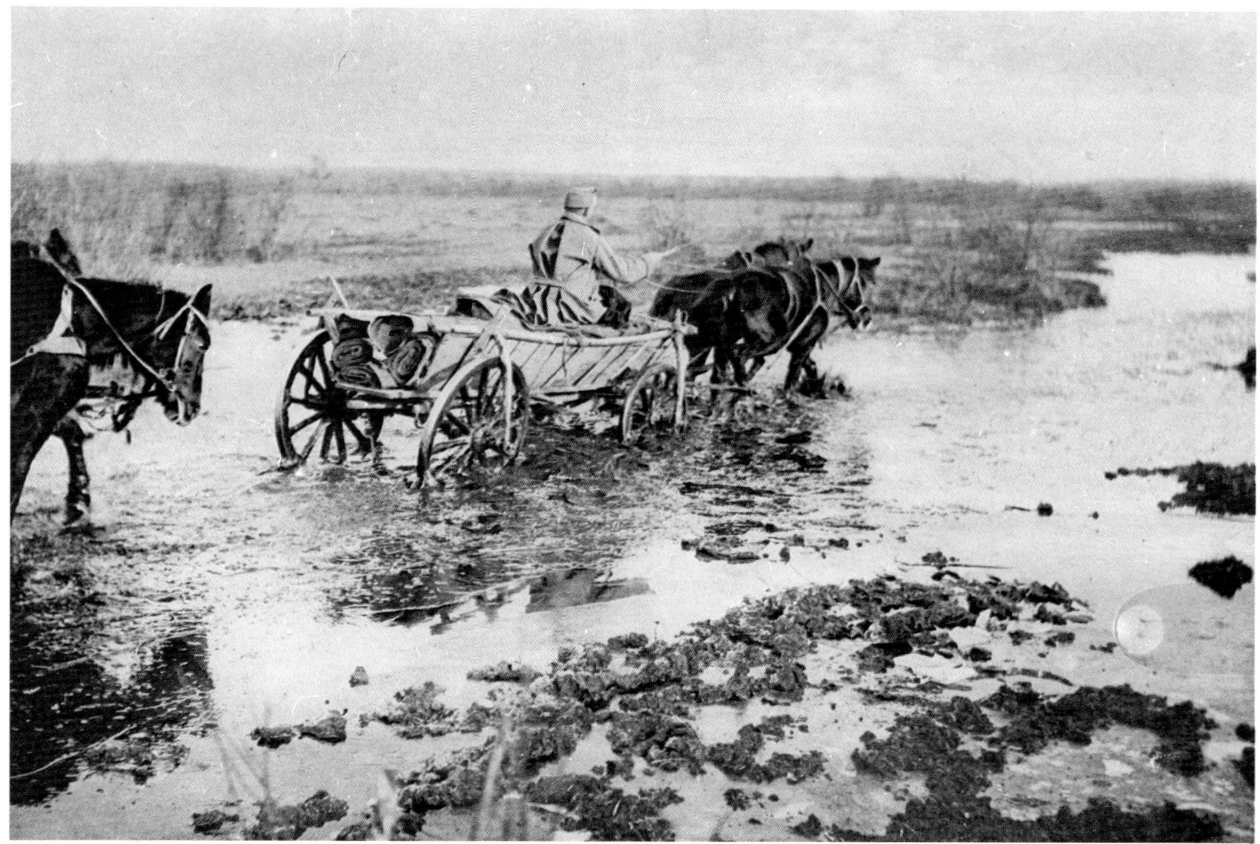

Lajos Fülle: *Deep in the Rokitno Marshes*

photographic collection of the majesty of our nation, the deeds, heroism, life, perseverance, heart and spirit of our people . . . throughout this long war, we have kept a record of events, from the first decorated troop train to the latest achievements of the Hungarian army'.

Such claims were not exaggerated. The War Albums of *Érdekes Úsjág* provide a consistent reflection of Hungarian society at the time, and a fascinating insight into its attitudes to war.

The Photographers

The photographers who entered for the competition came from all ranks of the army. Three were officers of the high command, including a colonel. There were three captains, four battery commanders, fourteen lieutenants and four second-lieutenants. From the lower ranks, there were one sergeant, one artillery sergeant, four cadets and two ensigns. There were also a superintendent, an artillery officer and an orderly officer.

It is impossible to estimate how many private soldiers sent in entries, as they were not credited in the captions, but there is one artillery gunner. One also finds doctors, veterinary surgeons, and a handful of professionals – the Vienna photographic agency Kiloph is well represented.

The Subjects

The majority of the photographs were taken near the battlefronts; Russian (thirty-seven pictures), Serbo-Montenegran (six) and Italian (seven). On the Russian front, the important battlefields were often associated with rivers. There are positions and trenches in Galicia, marshes at Rokitno, the gorge at Uszok. The photograph *Deep in the Rokitno Marshes*(above), shows the great effort required to fight in such marshes, which extend to 50,000 square miles. Here, damp and filth make it intensively difficult to move around and the horses in the picture are strained to the limits.

On the Italian front, there are pictures on Lakes Garda and Bolzano, in the Dolomites, and on the notorious River Isonzo. Among them, we find direct references to being at the very front line. The humorously titled *Where Are You, Italians?* (page 9) suggests a considerable assurance in the face of the enemy. *On the Adriatic* serves to illustrate that the sea, too, was a theatre of war. Scenes on the Serbo-Montenegran front are also often connected with rivers: the Drina, the Sava and the Danube. Two photographs depict scenes at Montenegran camps.

Cameras were still relatively cumbersome objects and their glass plates slow, so few photographs show actual fighting. Those that do present it as an exciting and masculine adventure. True, one could die in battle - but many survived. In general, however, the albums evoke war by showing men off duty (when it was in any case easier for them to take pictures), life in the trenches, the tools and weapons of war. Soldiers marching lent themselves particularly to photography and there are many pictures of 'our triumphant men' moving quickly and cheerfully.

There are several pictures of firing from trenches. Of course, one cannot see the enemy, any more than in the marching scenes. One senses he was far away, and that much of the war consisted of useless and sporadic shooting. Construction work was also a favourite (and safe?) subject. Against vast bridges (opposite), human figures seem diminutive, but they are heroic and ingenious – neither the enemy nor Mother Nature can stop the Hungarian soldier. We see him as master of bridge-building, cable-laying, First Aid, and driving horses.

Wars need weapons, and in the First World War they all seem to have been huge. The largest calibre gun of the time, the 30.5cm, bulky and vast (bottom right), is seen aimed at the sky like a mammoth telescope. A huge and ponderous battleship emits a cloud of thick white smoke as it lumbers through the water. A giant Zeppelin, being hauled from the sea where it has been shot down, looks like a stranded whale. Only an aeroplane, such a novelty that only one appears in the Albums, looks small and frail.

Many of the photographs show activities away from battle. There are, for instance, wounded soldiers. Not horribly wounded or mutilated, as these might not have been approved for publication. Their faces are usually hidden (for similar reasons?). When they can be seen, they eyes radiate calm: the Hungarian soldier, they suggest, endures his suffering stoicly. And he is always in good hands (below).

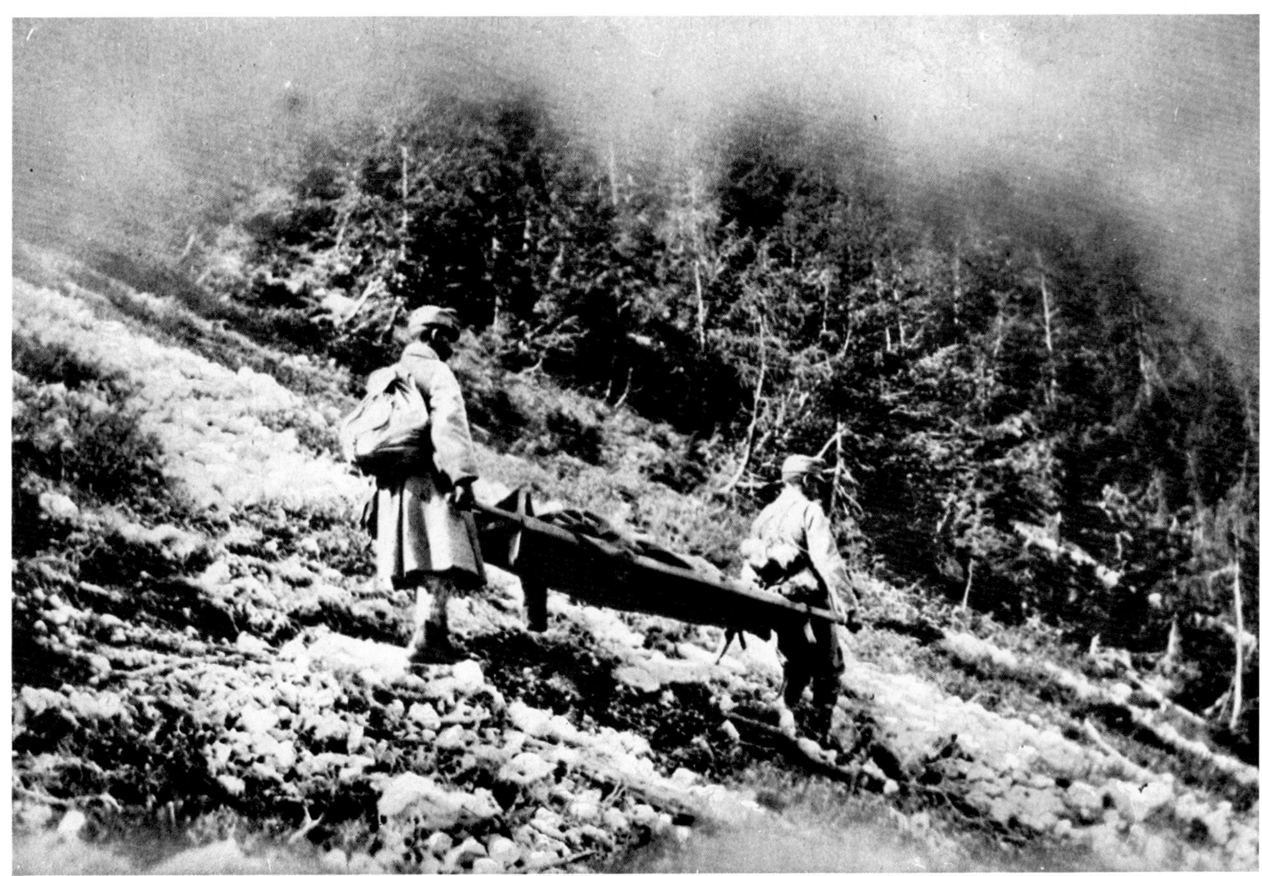

József Csanak: *Carrying the Wounded*

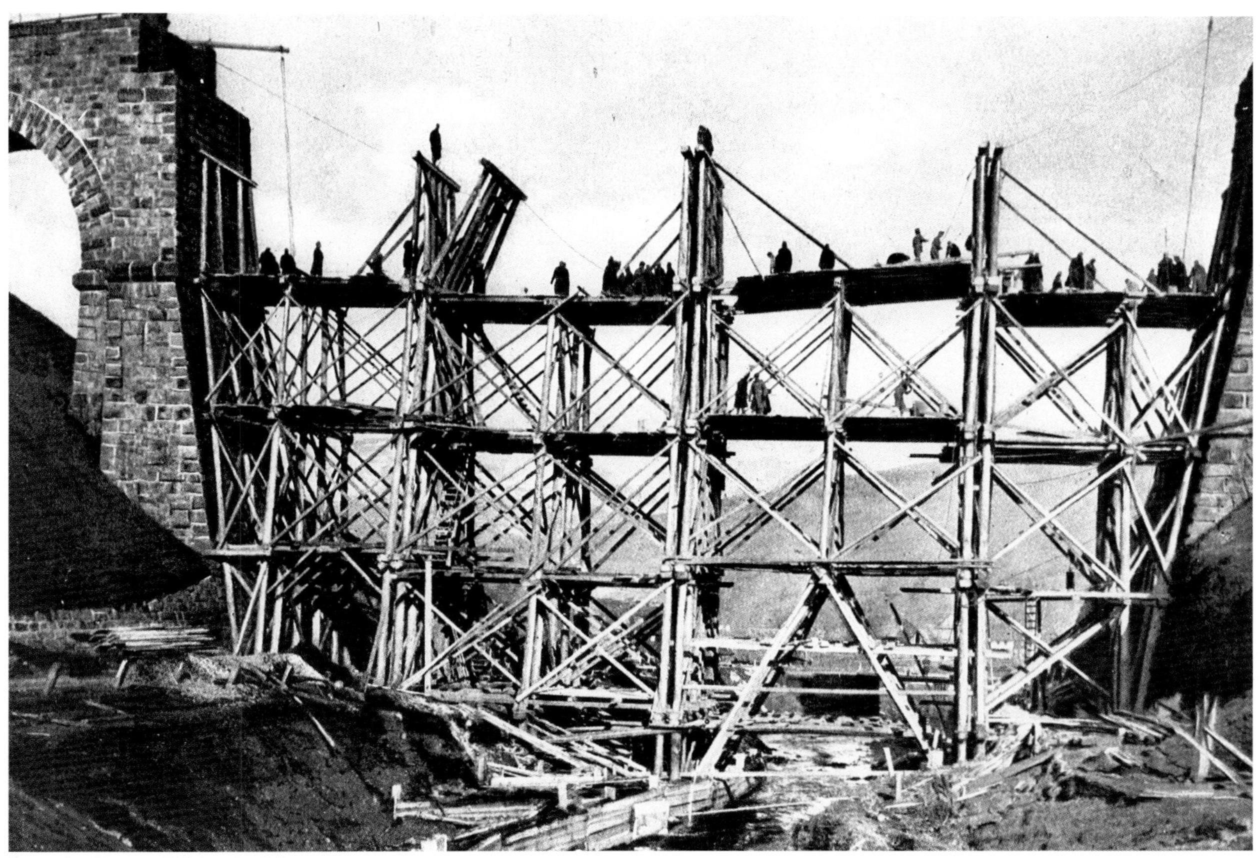

Gusztáv Aigner: *Bridge-building*

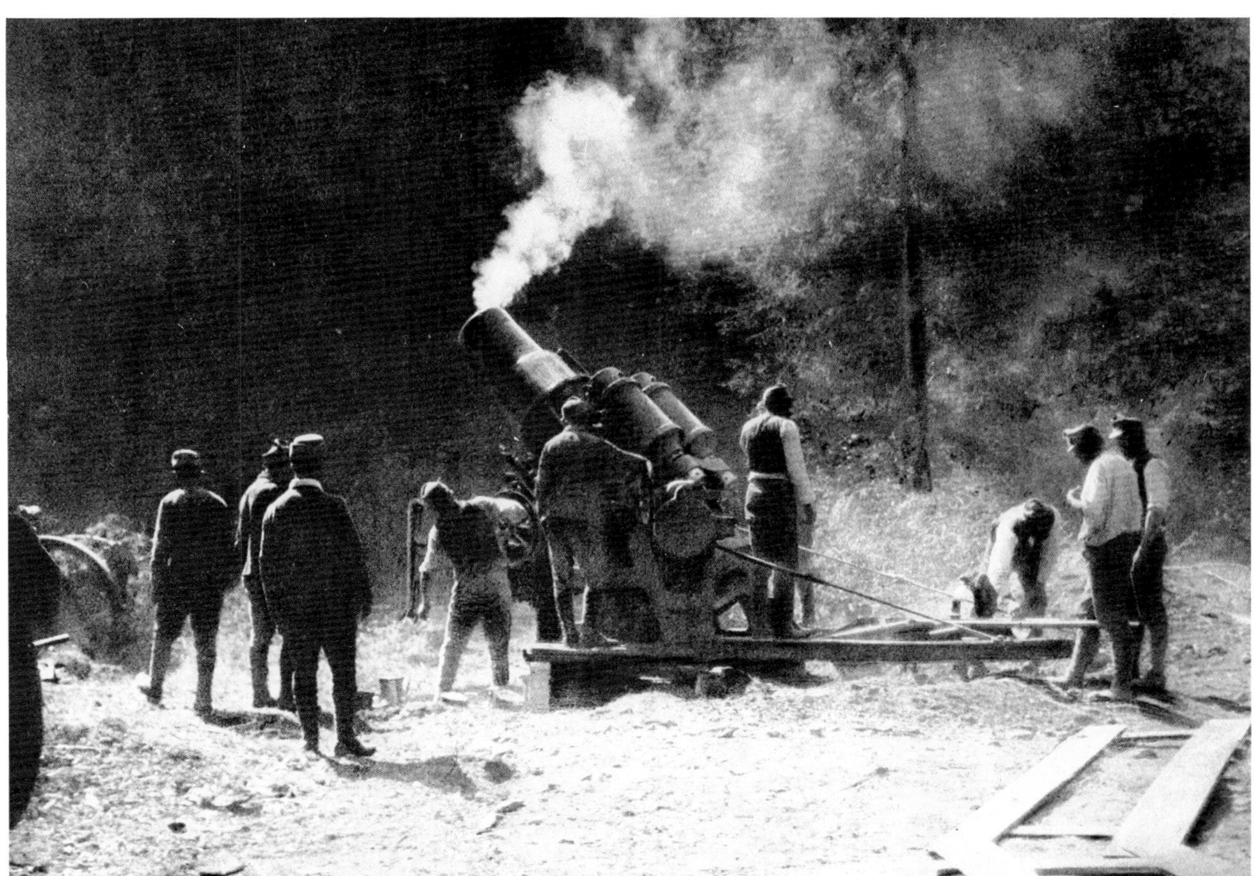

Rezső Csermák: *The 30.5 Cannon after Firing*

While on duty, soldiers are ceaselessly on vigil. Several photographs show solitary sentries: some apparently sad, on guard in an empty land, far from home and friends, others perhaps happy to be alone, to have time to think and to observe Nature. These pictures, and those of military patrols on mountain tops or among the forests, are among the most romantic in the albums (below).

When prisoners appear in the pictures, the soldiers are always Russian. Marching in long lines, their wrists chained or hand-cuffed, they are naturally tired and weary. Watched by their Hungarian captors on horseback, it is impossible to believe they have ever been energetic opponents. Captured civilians are shown in a more kindly light.

Even death cannot be avoided (opposite). On the battlefield, we are rarely shown more than two or three bodies in one picture, and there are always more enemies than Hungarians. The corpses look calm and peaceful, and the captions underline the dignity of death. Deaths in large numbers are represented by cemeteries, with row upon row of newly made graves. As these are usually in forests, the light is mysterious and overcast: perhaps there is a suggestion of life after death. The photographers show sympathy and compassion for dead animals and even for destroyed objects.

Many photographs – cheerful, and even amusing – show soldiers' life away from the fighting. They take time off for games, flirting with village women, playing with animals. They look happy, and seem to have plenty of time to be photographed. We see them bathing, eating, shaving, and so on in surroundings which seem neither particularly tidy nor military. Always, the captions underline the humour of the occasion; jokes and puns abound. It was exactly what the editors of *Érdekes Úsjág* wanted, for they did not want to frighten their readers at home. Even if their record were incomplete and distorted, they wanted it to show:

> *'The bright side of war . . . the unquenchable spirit of the Hungarian soldier even in the midst of the horror of war'.*

Only a few pictures showed the life of those who stayed behind: orphans, wives, parents, brothers, sisters. We see women doing what had previously been considered men's work, we see houses which have collapsed and left their owners homeless; most tellingly, we see the effect on children of deaths at the front. In *They Have Sent Everything Back, But Where is My Father?,* a little girl in white sits forlorn on a suitcase, holding a box full of medals. Such photographs as this and *The Orphans* are perhaps a little too obvious in their determination to wring pathos out of the situation, helped, once again, by the caption.

All in all, the War Albums of *Érdekes Úsjág* form a remarkable document. They had a great success at the time, and were endorsed by many important Hungarian personalities. Their rediscovery has been long overdue and will, we hope, make a powerful and moving contribution to *The Hungarian Connection*.

Gábor Szilágyi
(Translated by Erika László)

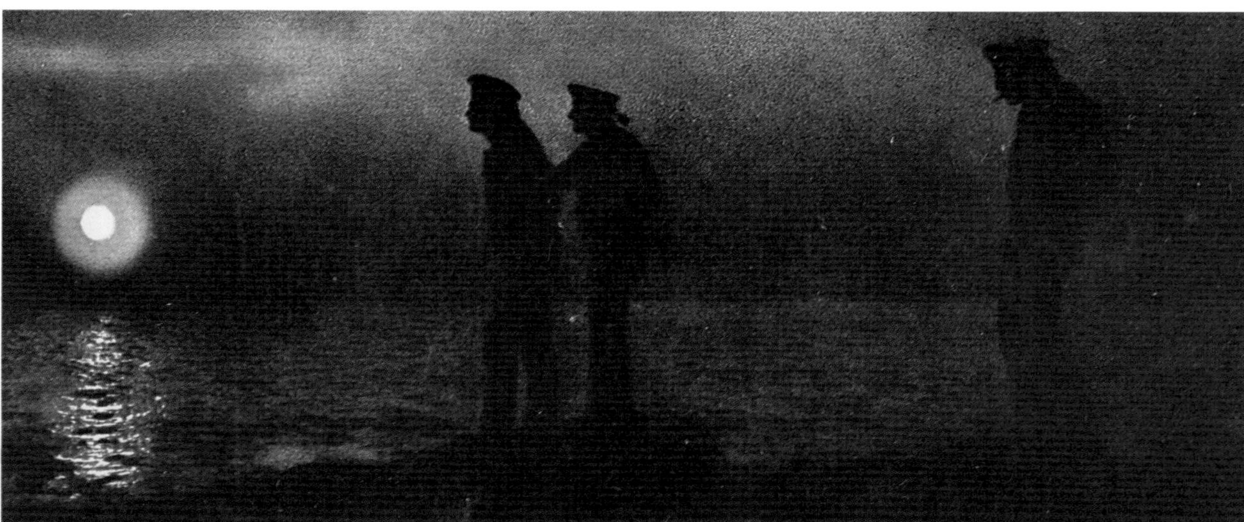

Emil Temesváry: *The Sailors' Night*

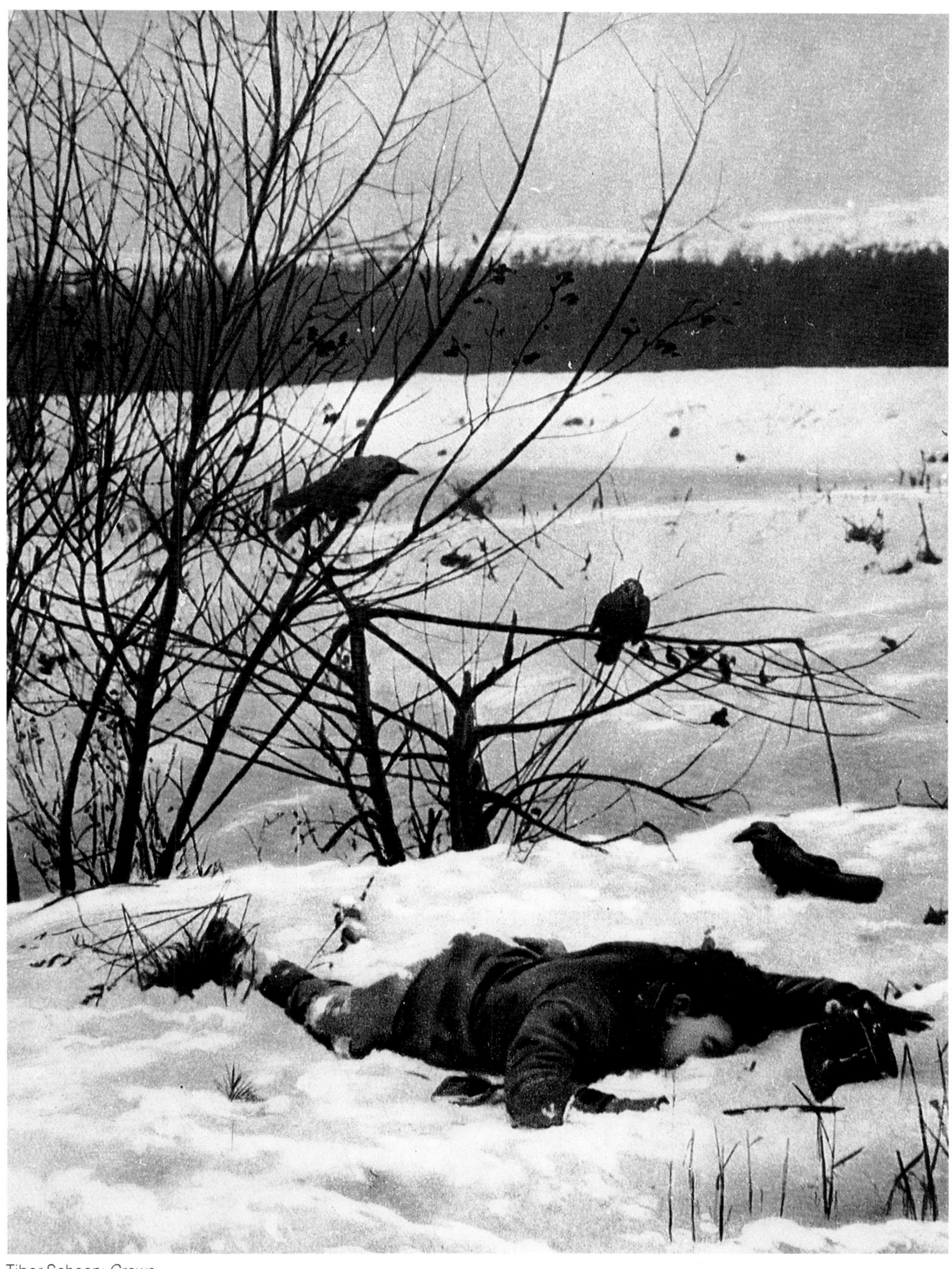

Tibor Schoen: *Crows*

Little Happenings

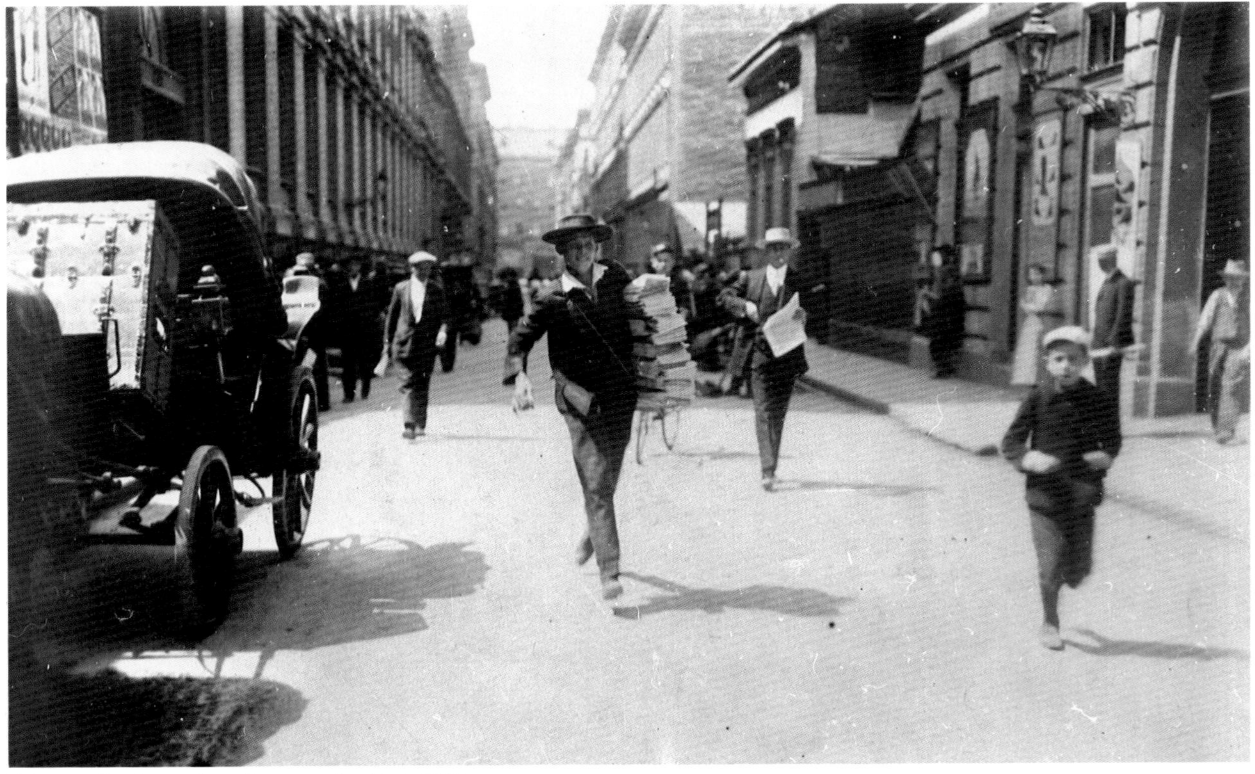

Unknown Photographer: *Newsvendor, Pest*, 1910s

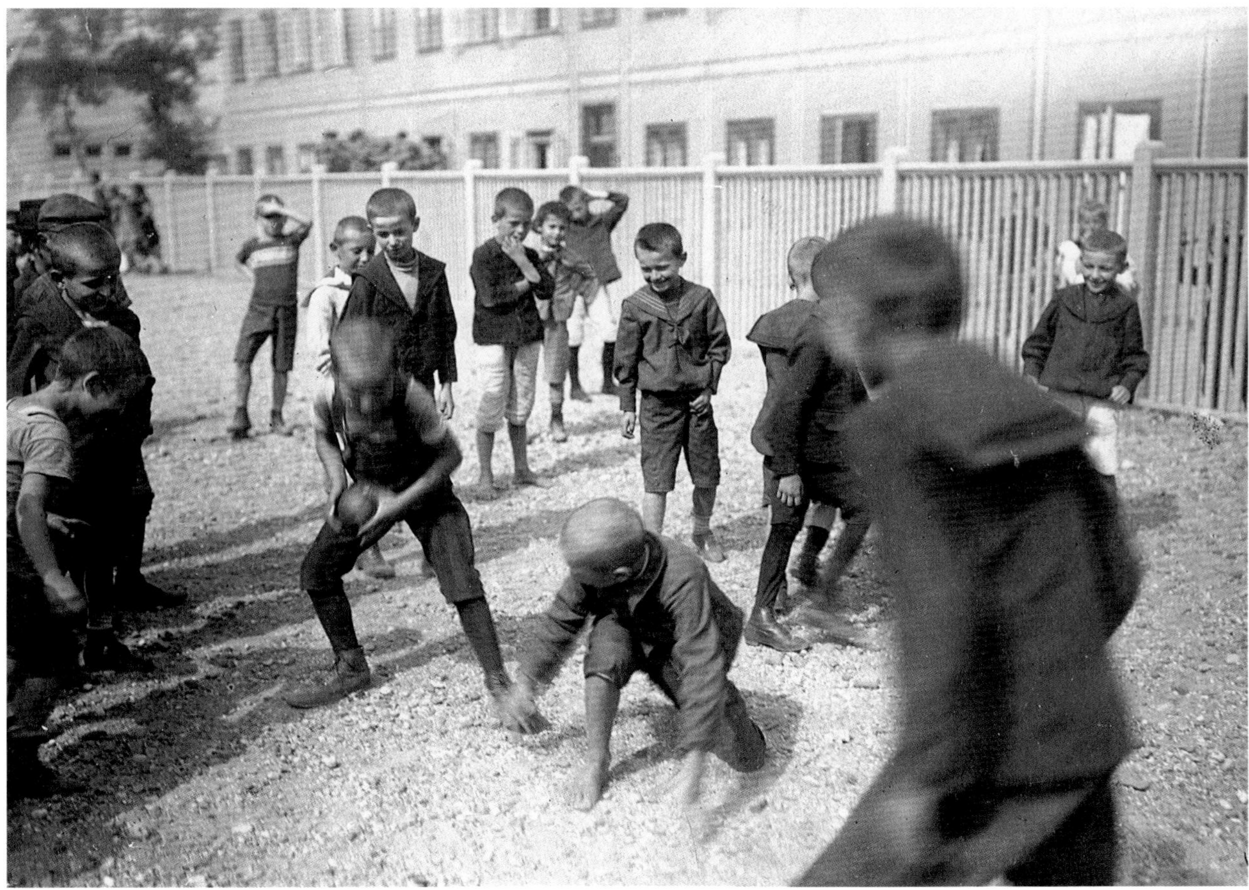

Mór Erdélyi: *Children Playing*, 1910s

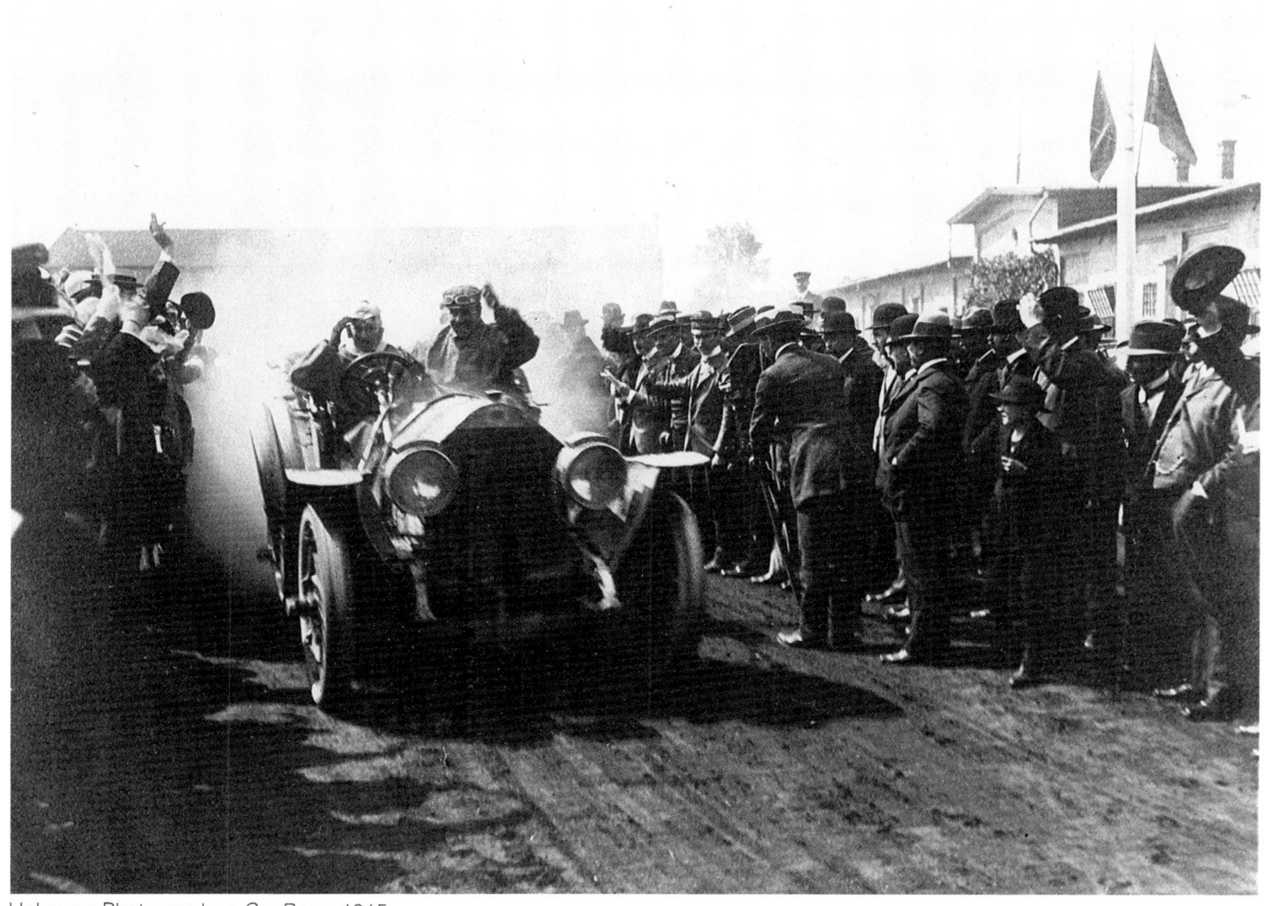

Unknown Photographer: *Car Race*, 1915

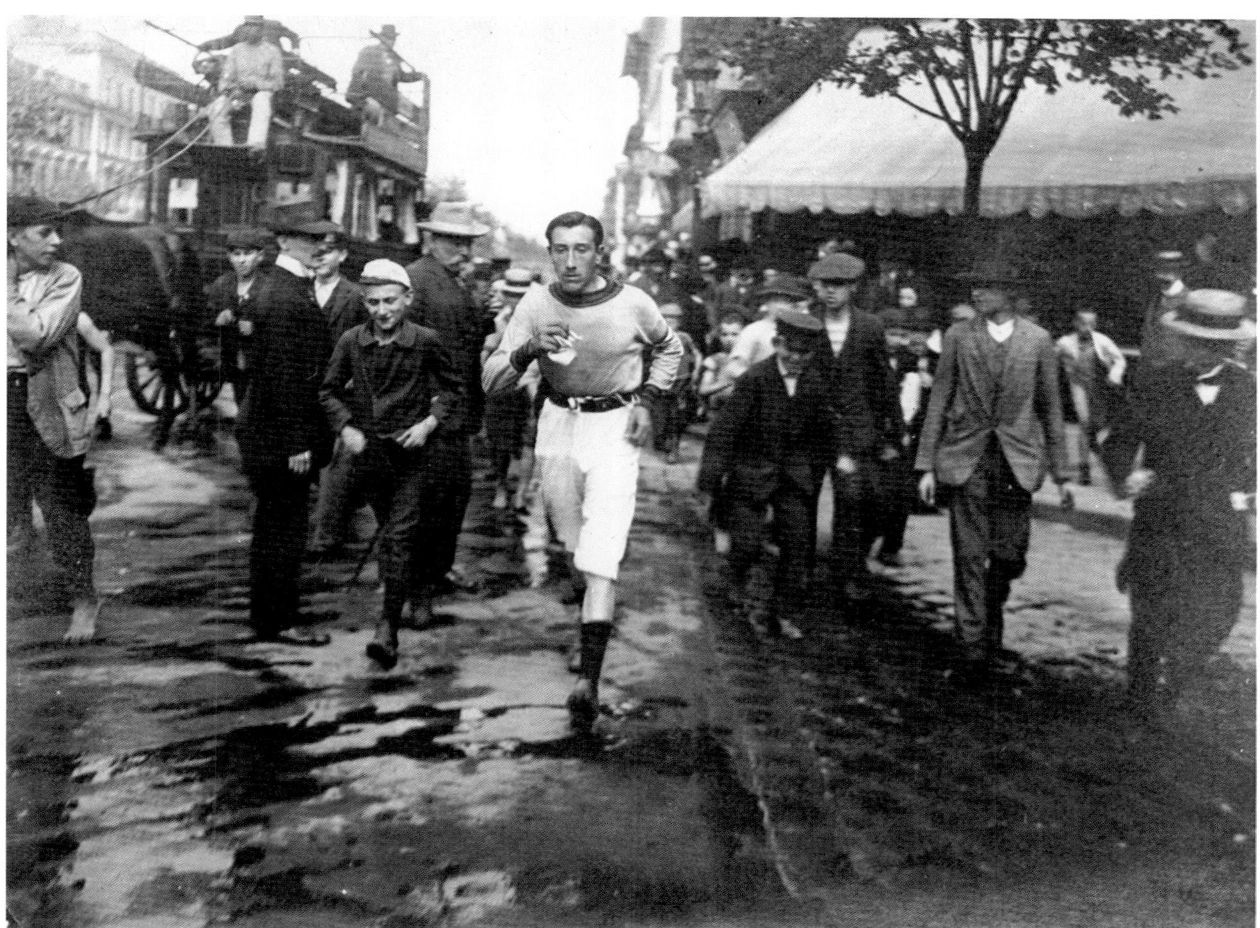

Unknown Photographer: *Foot Race*, 1910s

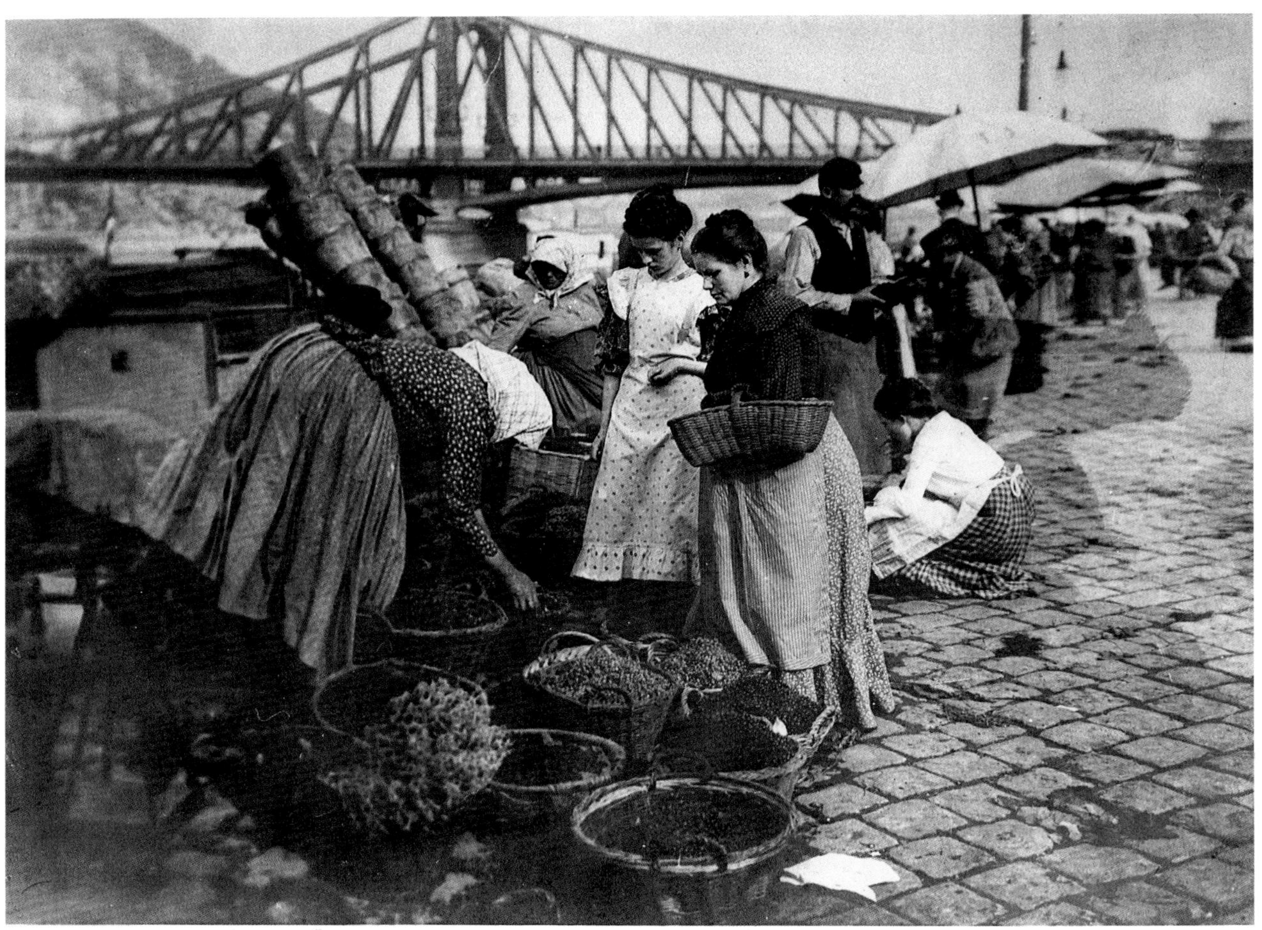

Rudolf Balogh: *Market on the Banks of the Danube,* 1906

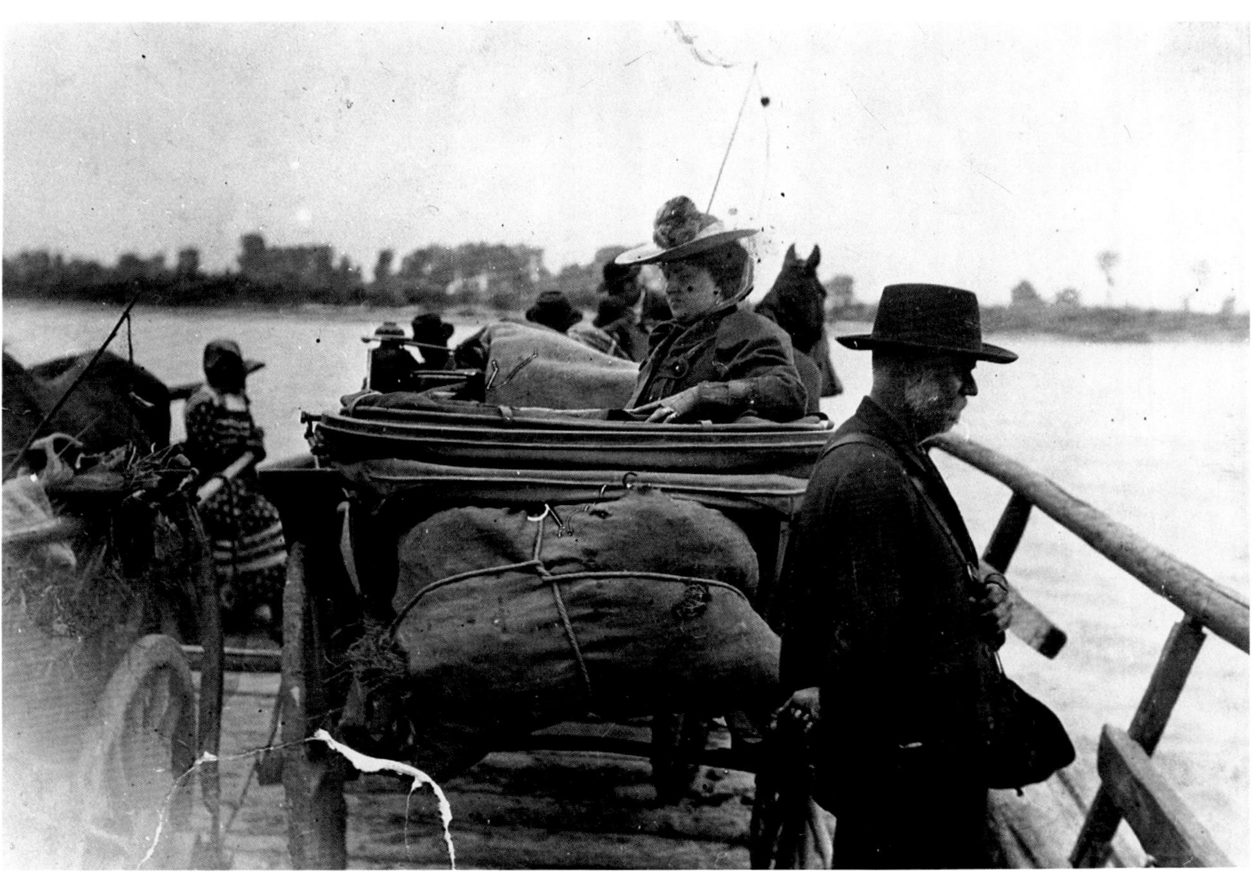

Akos Garay: *Danube Ferry Boat,* 1908

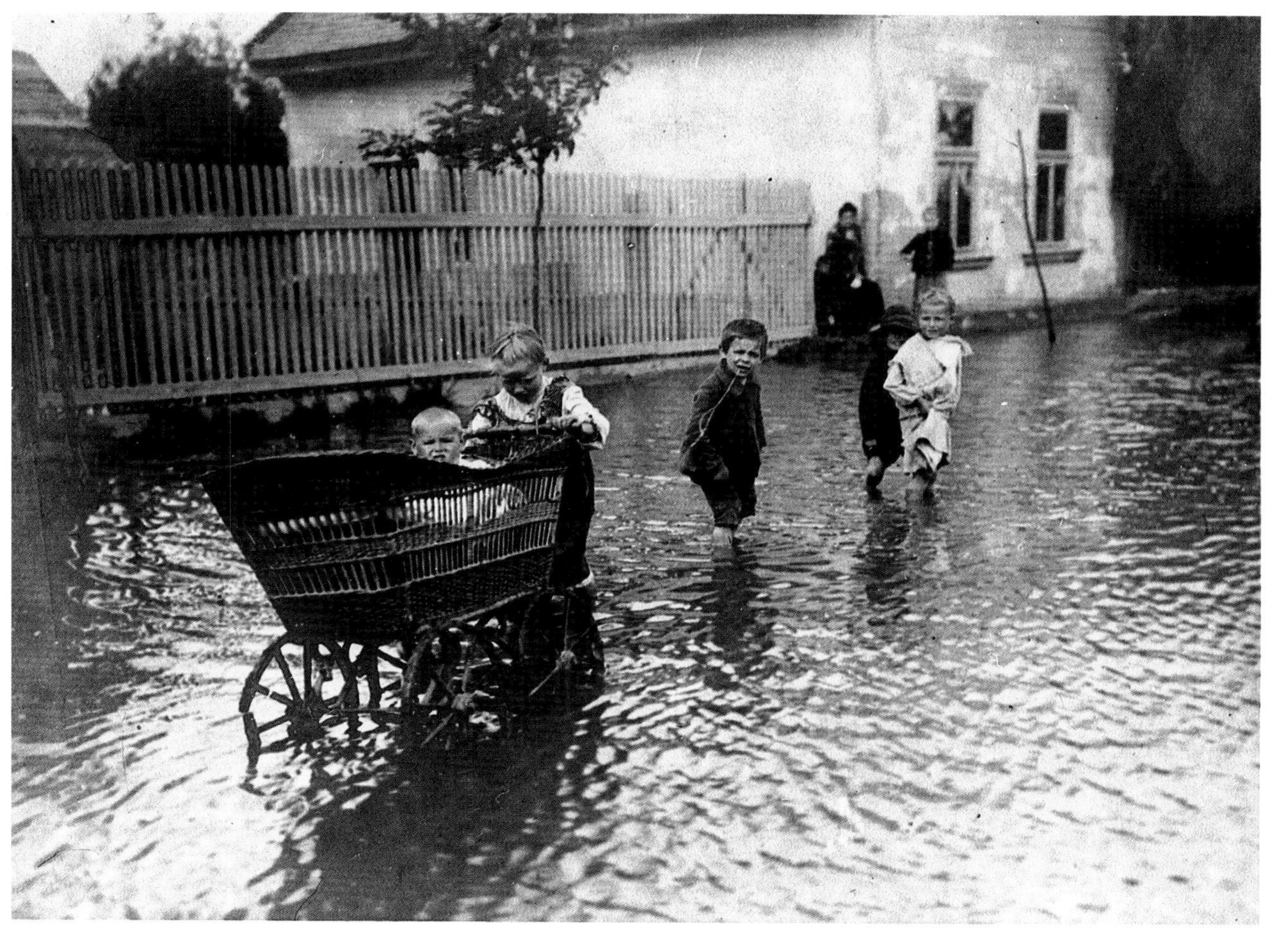

Rudolf Balogh: *Flood at Rákosszentmihály, Budapest,* 1906

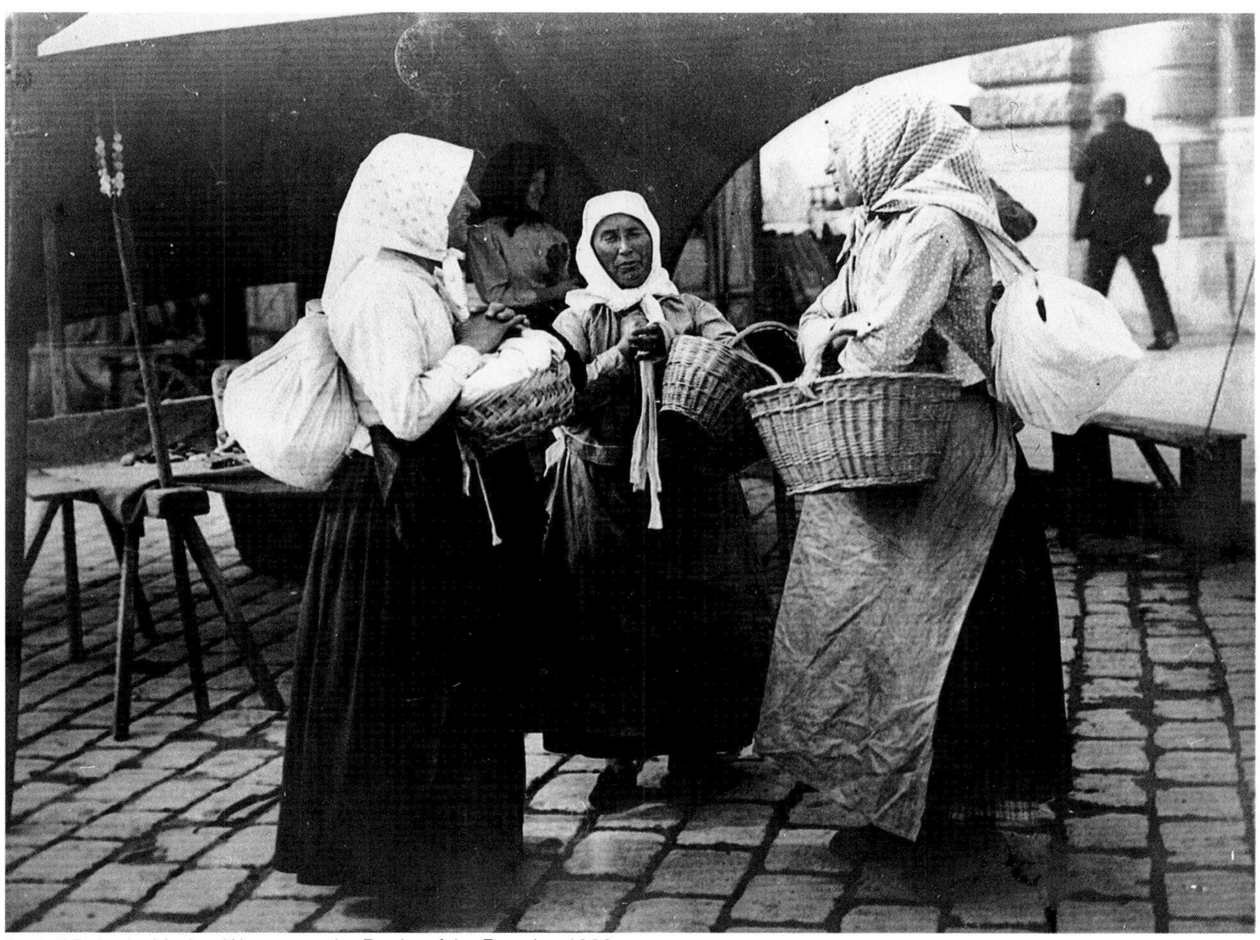

Rudolf Balogh: *Market-Women on the Banks of the Danube,* 1906

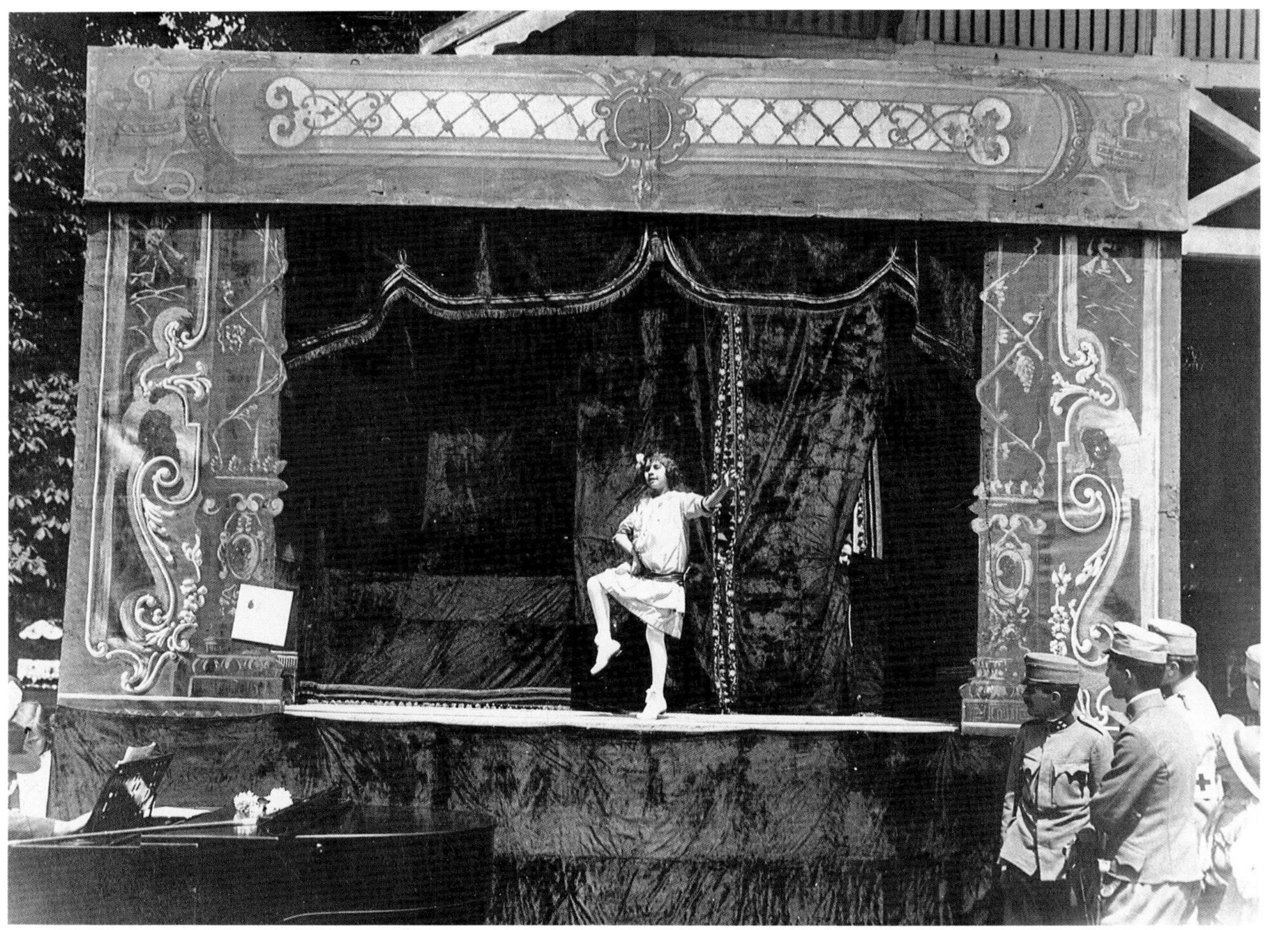

Unknown Photographer: *Child Artist,* 1915

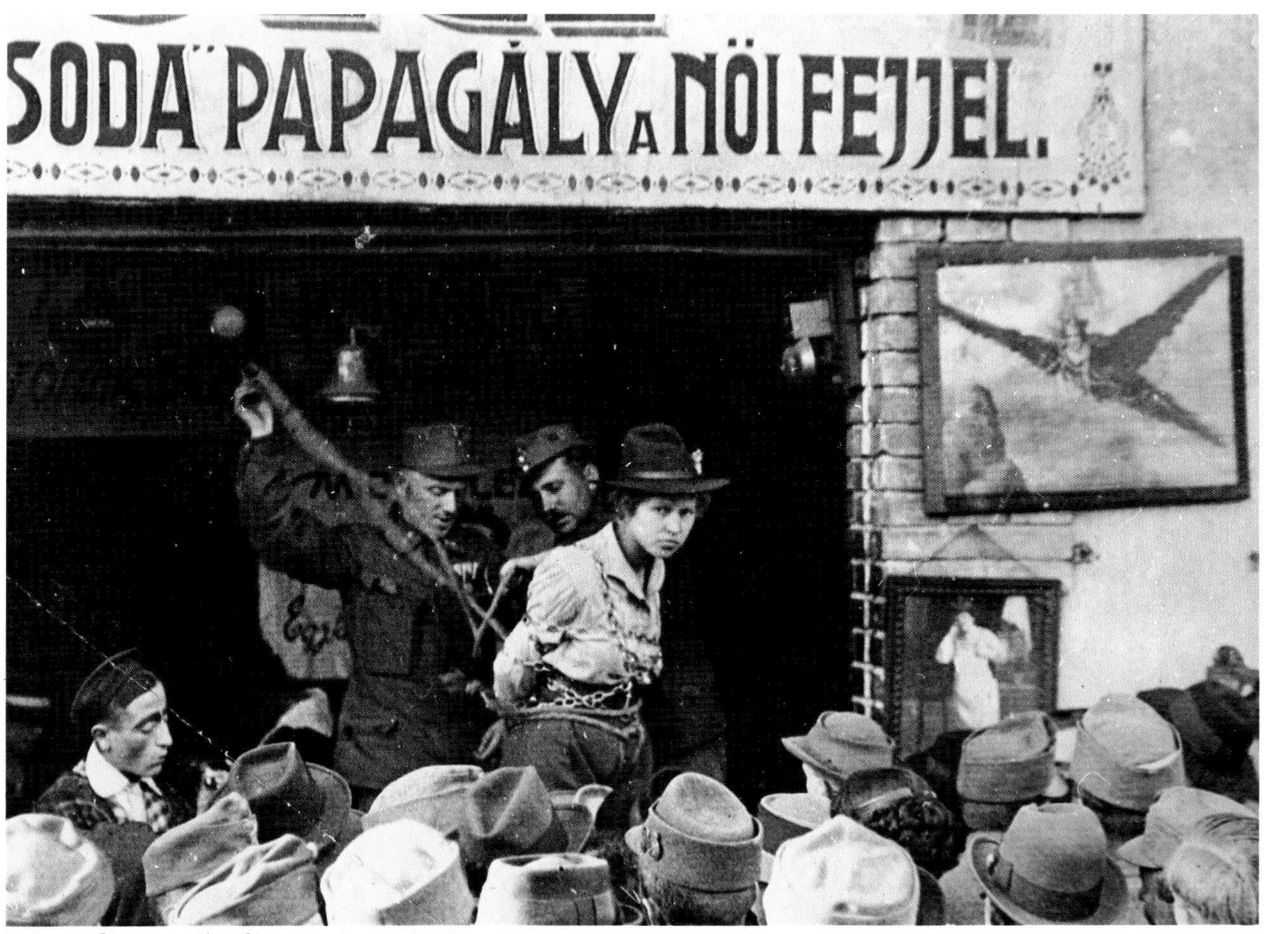

Unknown Photographer: *Showman in the Városliget, Budapest,* 1910s

János Müllner

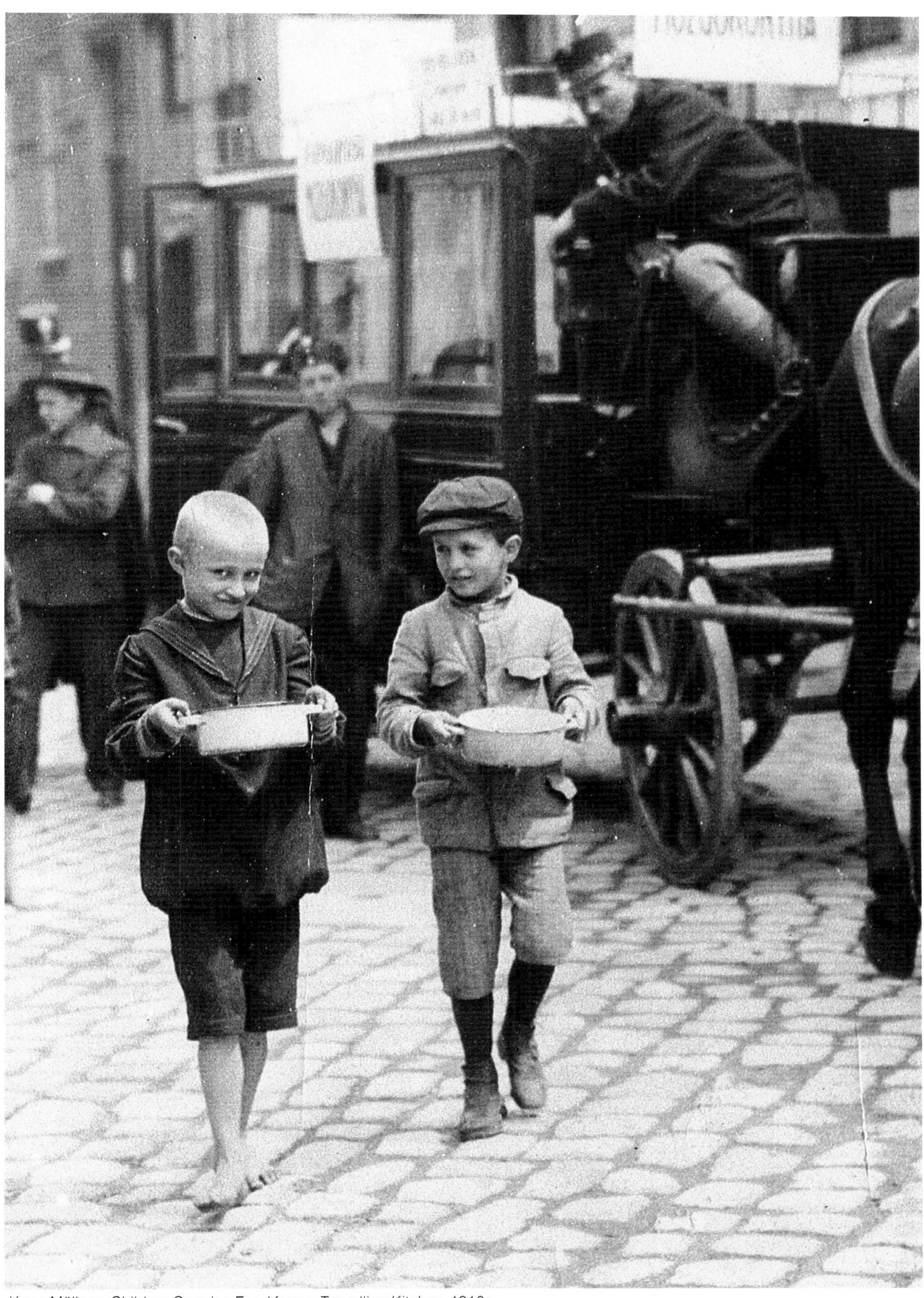

János Müllner: *Children Carrying Food from a Travelling Kitchen,* 1910s

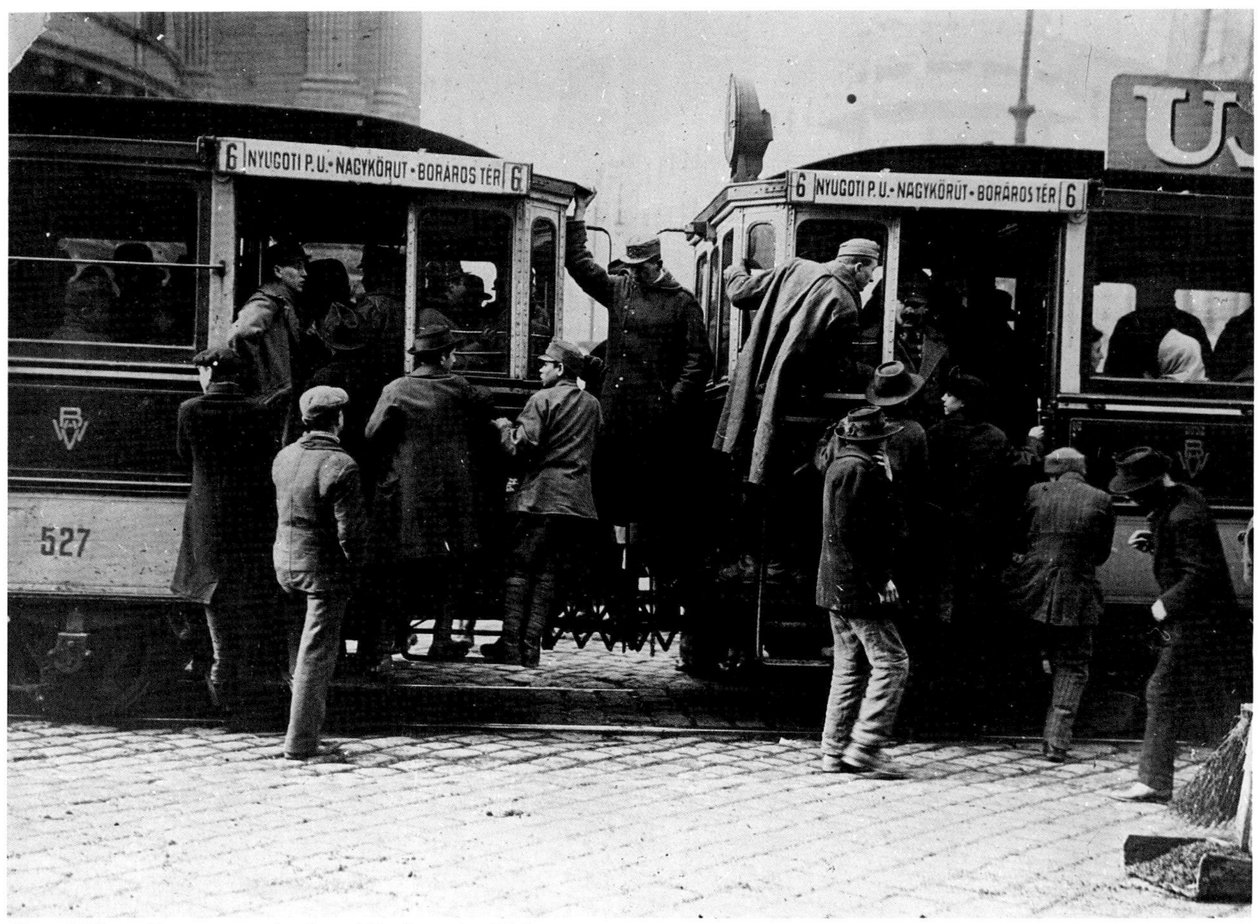

János Müllner: *Tramway on the Grand Boulevard*, c1917

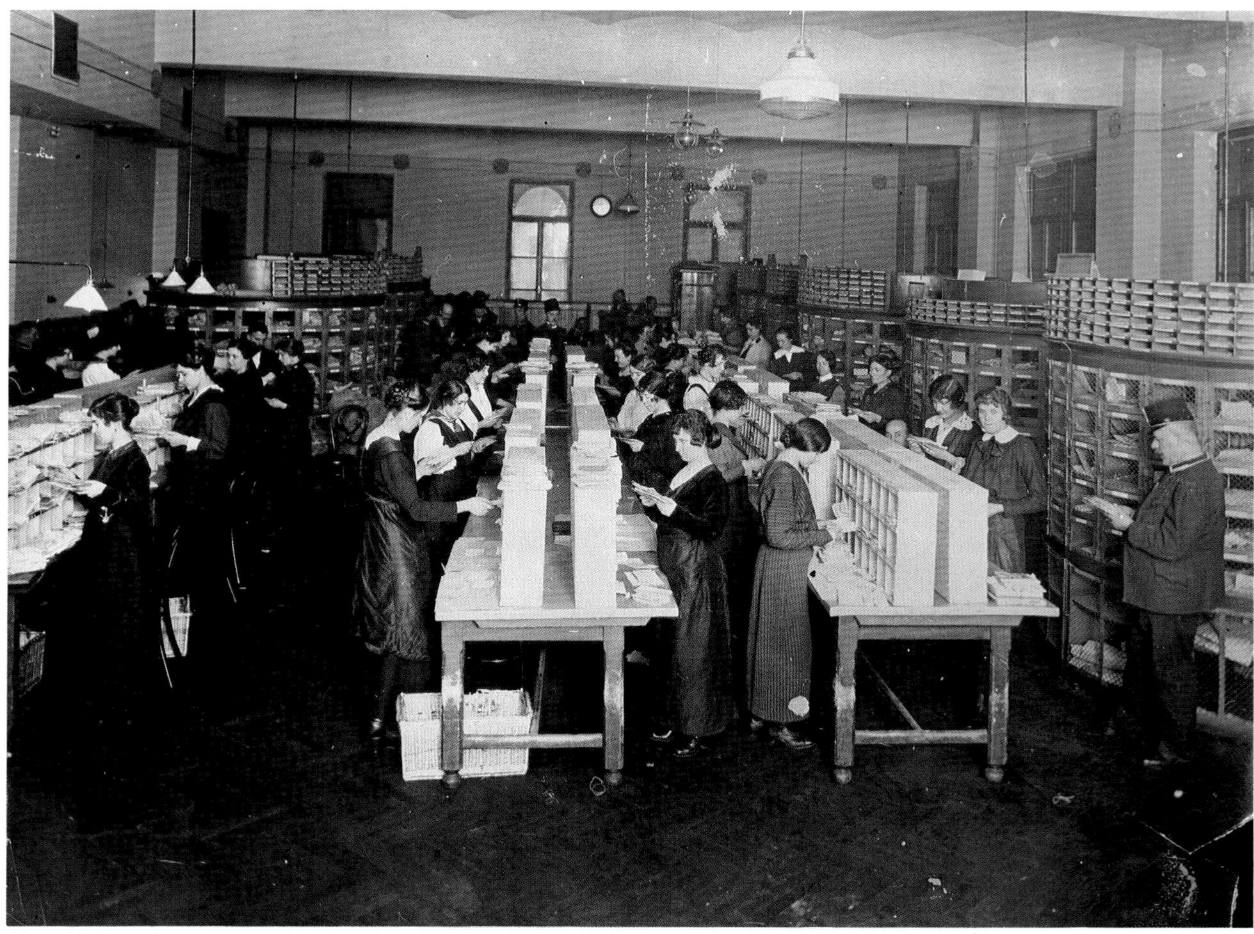

János Müllner: *Sorting Letters, Central Post Office, Budapest*, 1910s

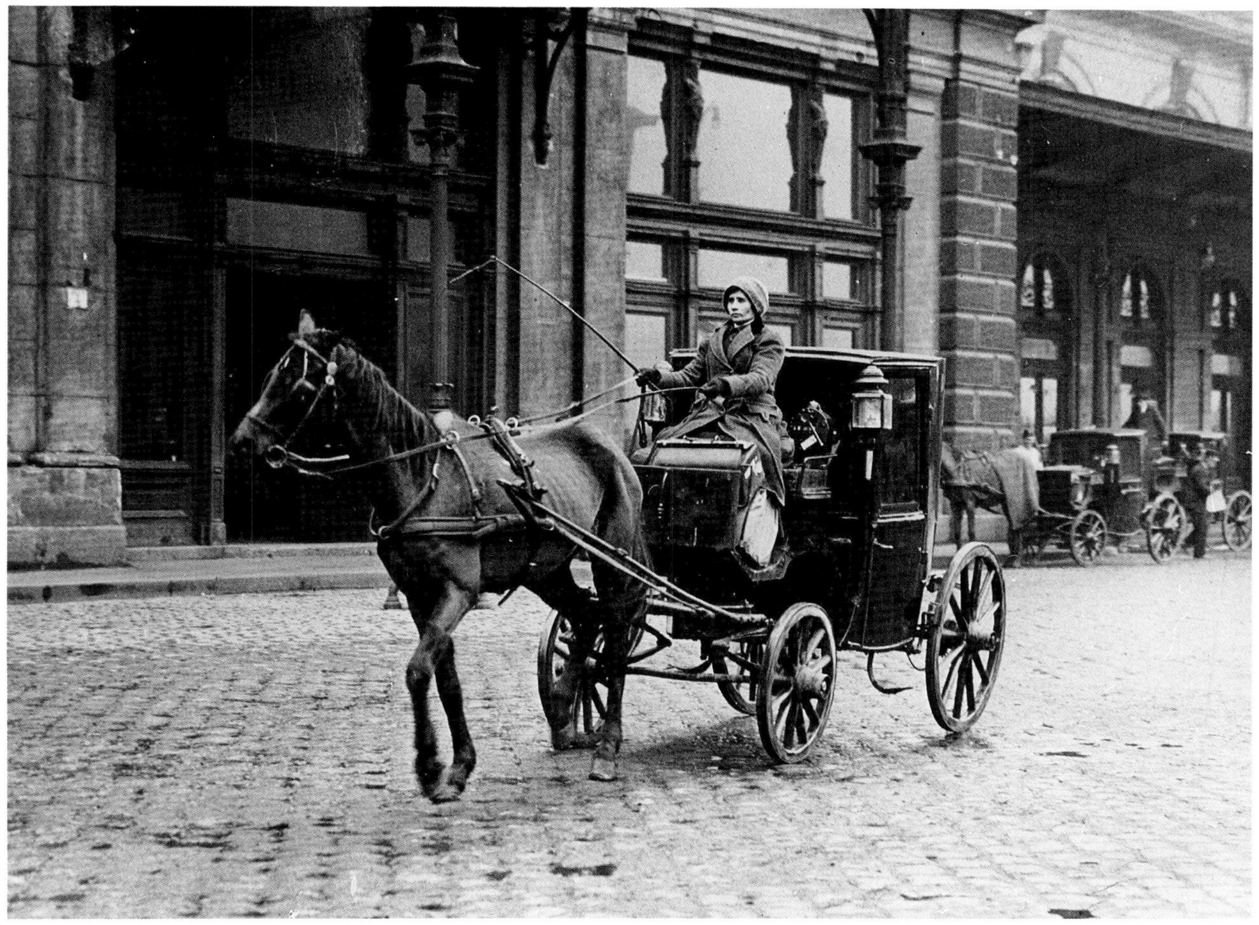

János Müllner: *Cabwoman, Budapest,* 1910s

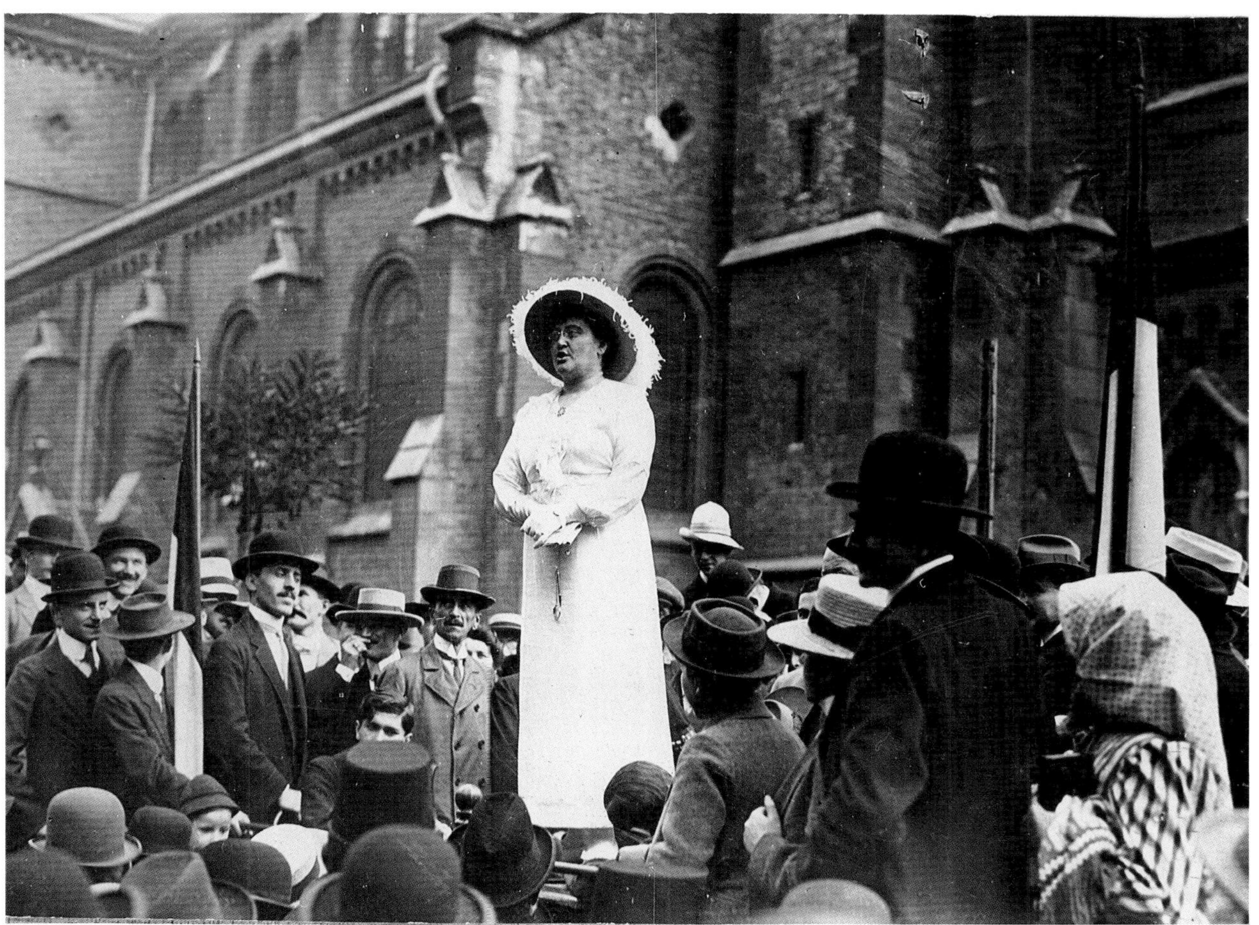

János Müllner: *Political Meeting, Budapest,* Summer 1913

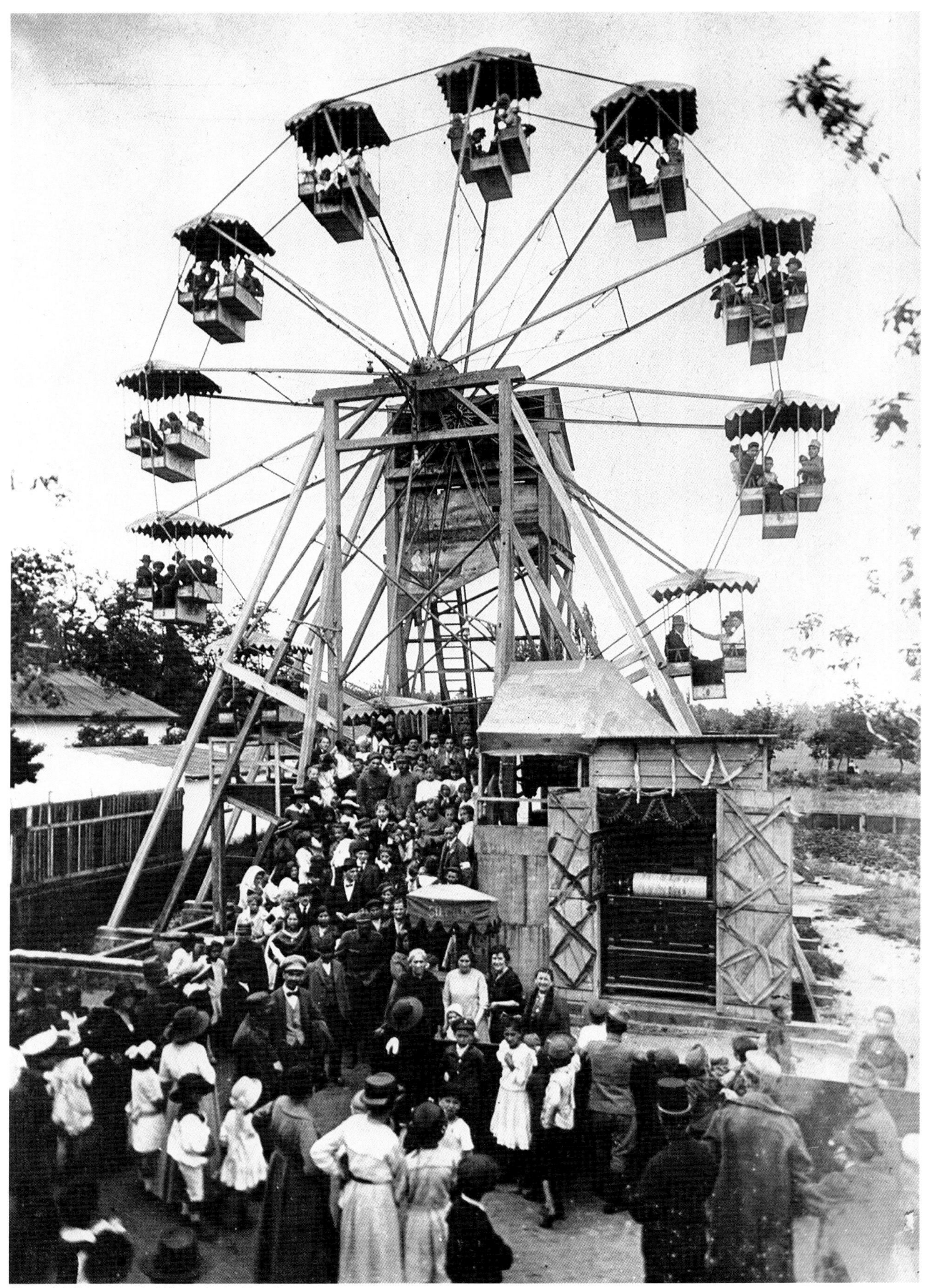

János Müllner: *Ferris-Wheel in the Public Park,* 1910s

János Müllner: Photojournalist

About a century ago, photography began to gain a new public prominence through its first appearances in the press. Throughout the 1880s, photographs began to make newspapers livelier than ever before, bringing credibility and authenticity to the written word by making readers feel they were witnessing the news 'with their own eyes'.

At first, newspapers reproduced photographs badly, and photography was in any case too slow to capture the speed and action of news 'as it happened'. But the introduction of high-speed shutters, fast dry plates and bromide film changed all this. By the early 1890s, engravings were being widely replaced by photographs, most notably in the most popular Hungarian weekly, the *Sunday News*. They were used for portraits of politicians, aristocrats and artists, for the exteriors of palaces and churches, for the interiors of drawing-rooms, libraries, and staircases.

More important was the coverage of events – in single photographs and in series. A wide readership was becoming familiar with press photographs, taking for granted the accurate and life-like detail with which they replaced the fuzziness of engravings. These new pictures needed new photographers – portraitists, designers; all with some other profession. Though they recognised the potential of press photography, they could not yet risk their old livelihoods in order to practise it.

One such, Mór Erdélyi,(see page 16, bottom), was destined for an unequalled distinction in Hungarian photographic history. Indeed, his achievement was rivalled only by a handful of photographers in other countries; Eugène Atget in France, Paul Martin in England and Heinrich Zille in Germany. By the turn of the century, a whole generation of press photographers was growing up around Erdélyi, of whom the leading and most important member was János Müllner (1870-1925).

Even today, comparatively little is known about Müllner's life, personality and work. His surviving photographs in public collections, all apparently taken between 1904 and 1919, offer some evidence. Each is stamped 'János Müllner, Photo Illustrator', with an unfashionable address in a working-class quarter. As there are no portraits, *cartes de visite* or cabinets, we can assume he did not have a studio.

The life of ordinary people seems to have been a major impulse for much of Müllner's animated and ingenious output Before newspapers regularly commissioned press photographers, he was a freelance, using his true reporter's instincts to seek out the most important social and political events, and always managing to find the best viewpoint.

Müllner's remarkably modern results were achieved with the heavy and cumbersome cameras of his time, taking glass negatives ranging in size from half plate (9cm x 12cm), through full plate (13cm x 18cm), to 18cm x 24cm. His positives, all made by contact printing, are typically glossy, with strong contrasts, a wide range of tonal values, and few of the reddish tones found in many other prints of the time.

Müllner's earliest known photograph, taken in 1904, shows a ceremonial public funeral – that of Mór Jókai, great novelist of the age, with mourning crowds on the steps of the National Museum. Five years later, he photographed another such ceremony at the same spot, the re-interment of the ashes of the legendary Lajos Kossuth, leader of the 1848 War of Independence. In between the two, he recorded political meetings, their breaking up by the police, and demonstrators for universal suffrage thronging Parliament Square.

The time was ripe for photojournalism. Hungarian social and political life was undergoing great changes, and Müllner was always on hand to capture them. In 1908, he photographed evicted families camping on the street and meetings of desperate tenants protesting at extortionate rents. There were more demonstrations in favour of universal suffrage, in 1911 at the Museum of Fine Arts, and in 1912 at the National Museum, where Müllner photographed Count Tivadar Batthány addressing the crowd, before going with them to the Millenary Monument in the City Park.

On the outbreak of World War I in June 1914, Müllner photographed soldiers preparing for active service, but he spent the next few years recording the impact of war on Budapest and her citizens. His pictures show us slippers being made for use in military hospitals, people in the streets anxiously awaiting news from the front, vegetables being grown in what had once been the National Riding School's ice rink, school-boys working in the fields, an aristocratic woman distributing sweets to the troops. In a particularly impressive photograph of wounded soldiers recuperating on the hospital ship *Augusta*, Müllner's strong composition compresses the soldiers between the silhouette of the ship's funnel in the right foreground and the dark shape of its whistle on the left.

The more seriously wounded are in military hospital, where Müllner records the wards, kitchen, and store room as well as soldiers being bandaged. On a hospital train, he photographs the shiningly clean laboratory and operating theatre. War Relief offices are set up, widows and orphans learn to sew; the Red Cross Committee of Budapest girls' school mends clothing for soldiers. Clothes are transported, saucepans are melted down for weapons, more – and younger – troops are enlisted, horses are trained (outside the public cemetery). Children play war games and have medical examinations before going on free summer holidays. The soup kitchen in front of the Opera Comique and the tug-of-war and sausage-eating competitions on Margaret Island, Budapest's traditional playground, are reminders that some aspects of life are unchanged, even in wartime.

In 1916, the death of Franz József shook the monarchy to its foundations. The swearing-in of his successor, Charles IV, and his wife Zita, becomes Müllner's most ambitious undertaking. In a total of thirty-nine photographs, fifteen are of the Coronation procession and are taken from one viewpoint. The rest show the audience at a promenade concert given in the king's honour, policemen on Castle Hill, crowds hoping for a sight of the crown, soldiers selling badges with the king's monogram. The parade is rehearsed, stands are built for spectators, a dais and triumphal arches are constructed. Müllner rushes through the crowds, avoiding carts, jumping into cabs, always finding the best places to set up his tripod. The result is a comprehensive and genuine series.

The war ended in 1918. Discharged troops hurried home from the front and in the autumn the 'bourgeois revolution' broke out. Müllner was in the streets – where else? – photographing the scenes in Parliament Square when the Republic was proclaimed, an officers' demonstration, posters on empty shop-windows, soldiers crowding onto buses. The following spring, when the 'proletarian revolution' led to the proclamation of a Hungarian Socialist Republic, Müllner again provides an authentic record. Always, his pictures reveal personal dramas among momentous events and always, however hastily they must have been made, look as if he had hours, or even days, to contemplate and construct them.

In these memorable 133 days, grave and amusing events are intermingled. Politicians make speeches; soldiers wait for a train or take part in a cycle race; policemen are killed in street fighting and buried; children listen to a story and a lecture on the evils of alcohol, or set out on their first vacation. Müllner's photographs of these are dramatic *tours de force*, capturing essential truths, and often making us smile.

The tension in *A Woman Cabdriver* (page 23, top) come from Müllner's careful choice of viewpoint, which controls the composition and the strong diagonal movement of horse and cab. This viewpoint, too, brings a dynamism and animation to *Ferris Wheel in the Public Park* (page 24). In *Mass Meeting* (page 23, bottom), the bulky figure of the speaker is emphasised by being photographed from below, and the strong contrast almost dissolves the fine feathers of her hat into fibres. In *Fairy Tale Programme at the Museum of Social Sciences* , the expansive geometrical form again comes from a diagonal composition. The foreshortening peculiar to this is seen to particular effect in *Dress Market in Dohany Street*, where the piled pyramids of old clothes might make no sense seen from a lower angle. At the top of the picture, the perspective is closed off by three storeys of corridors; at the bottom, there is an open view into the street. This feeling that the subject stretches out beyond the confines of the photographs is also seen in *Restaurant on Margaret Island*, where the high-lights of the white tablecloths and the light-coloured hats are almost pointillist.

It is not surprising that the high viewpoint becomes virtually Müllner's trademark. In *Coach-yard at the Prime Minister's Residence, New Year's Day 1917*, we see countless cabs from above, with a lifeless gas lamp defining the foreground and an empty grandstand the rear. Movement comes from scurrying passers-by and depth from the viewpoint, which makes the diagonals intersect at the very point where the palace meets the grandstand.

Even Müllner's snapshots show this care and formality. In *Teenage Girls on Margaret Island*, for instance, two girls in white dresses move with clumsy grace, watched by a soldier on a raised stage in the background. To one side, a man looks out of the picture, laughing boisterously at something unseen. These four apparently unconnected figures are locked into a diagonally and horizontally ordered composition. Whichever one we choose to look at, our eye is drawn to the next. In *Spectators at the Berlin-Budapest Football Match*, the shapes themselves become the organising features. The spectators near the camera are full of character; further off, they become faces and hats; further off still, they are mere spots, declining into an abstract mass.

Gábor Szilágyi
(Translated by Julianna Vidor)

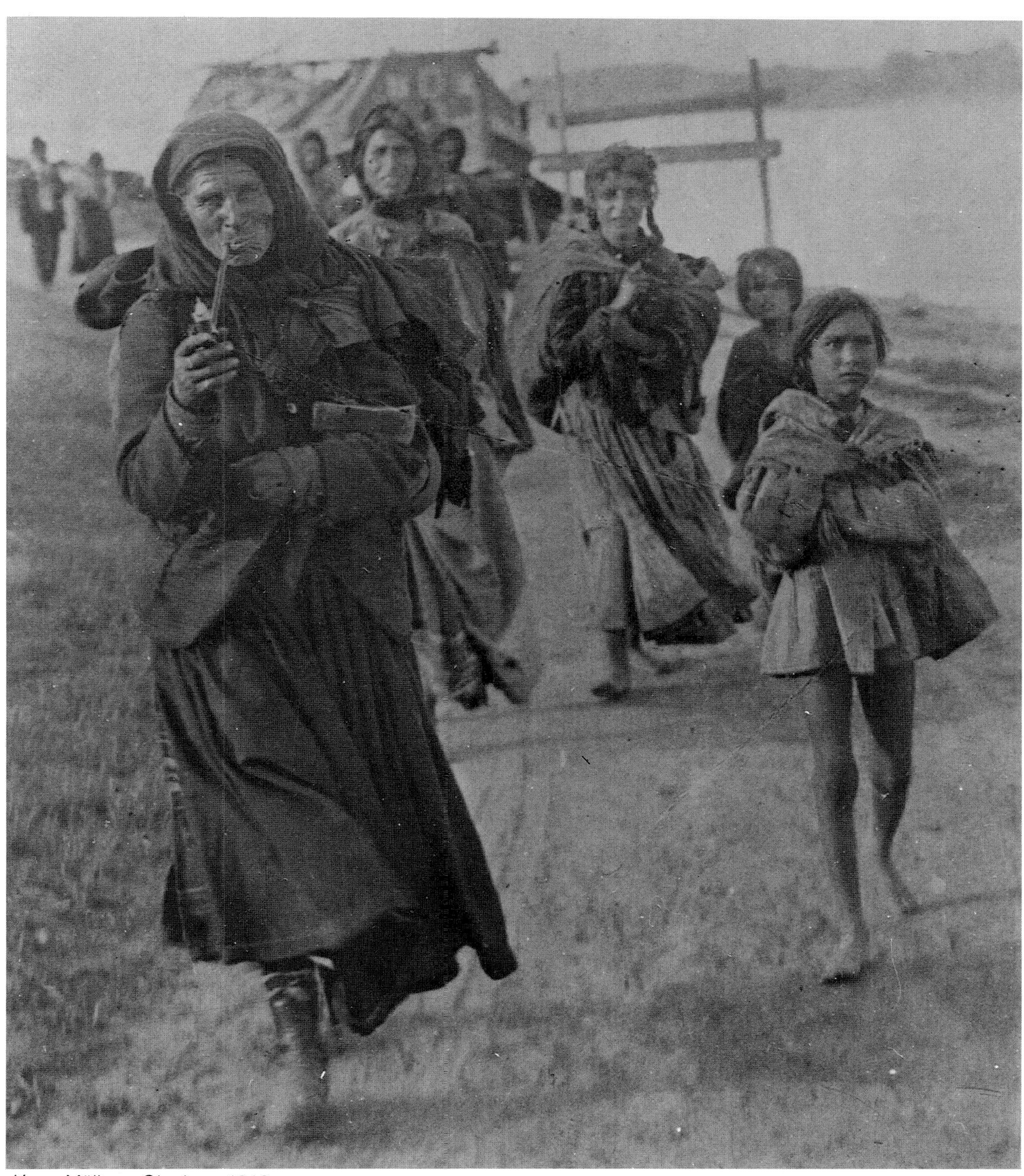

János Müllner: *Gipsies*, c1912

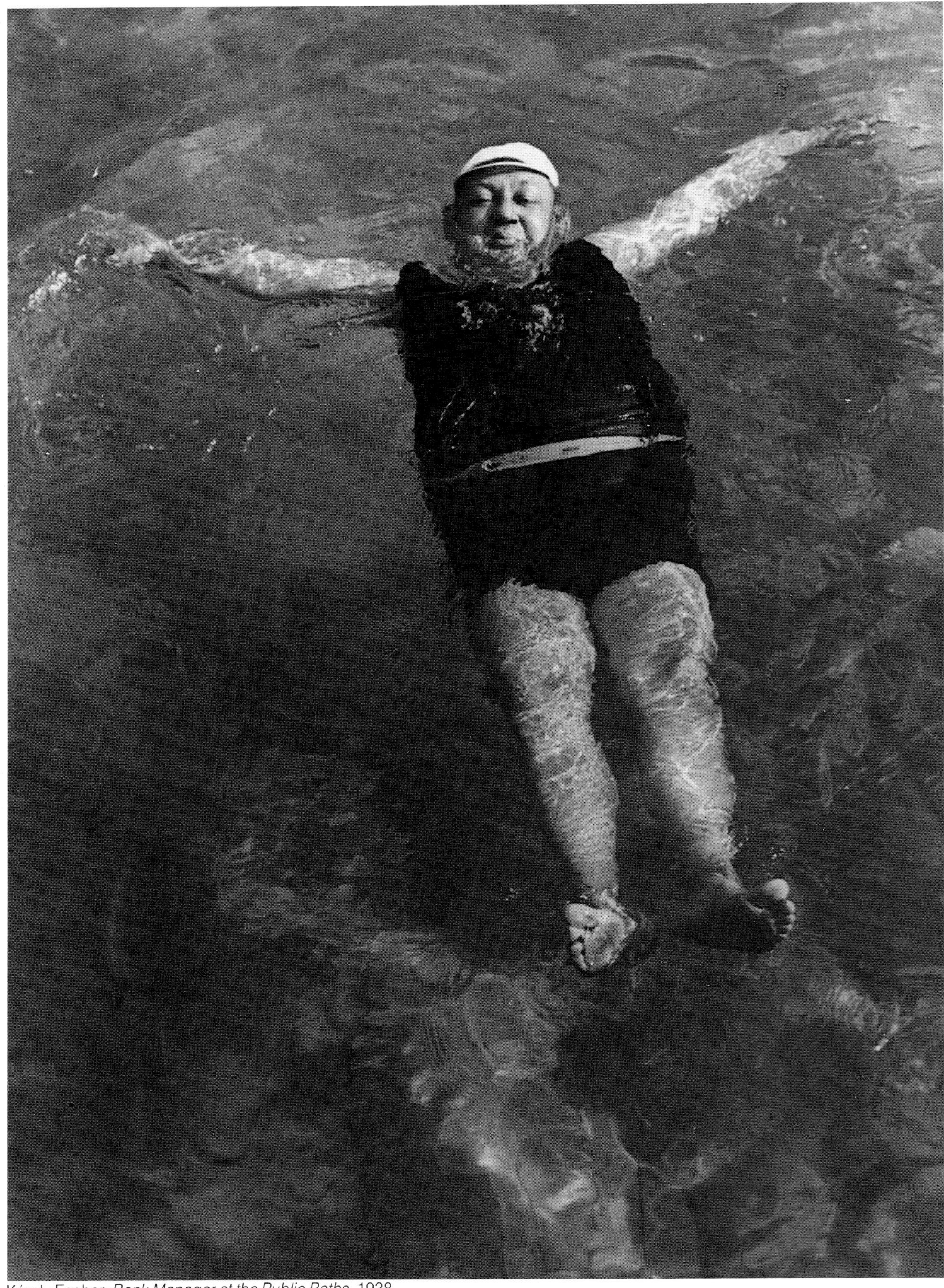

Károly Escher: *Bank Manager at the Public Baths*, 1938

Károly Escher

Károly Escher (1890-1966) was one of the outstanding personalities of Hungarian photography, a leading figure of photojournalism in his time. Hardly influenced by traditions, precedents or foreign trends, he developed a new style of photojournalism. Though he refused to be called a photographic artist, he advanced photojournalism to the rank of an art, proving that news can be depicted artistically, not merely reported and recorded. While expressing a reporter's moral and aesthetic views, he could at the same time elicit an intellectual and emotional response. His artistic sense adds aesthetic value to his work; it also enables him to address universally valid issues through a single event.

Károly Escher was born on October 21 1890, in Szekszárd, a small town in Southern Hungary with rich cultural traditions. Later, he moved with his parents to Budapest, where he finished four years of elementary school. In his 1959 book *Riportfényképezés* ('Photographic Journalism') he tells how he chose his profession, describes his many experiences and achievements as an artist-reporter, and alongside this personal account of his life, shows a cross-section of his work. He knew he was born to be a photojournalist: 'It was very difficult for me to find my way; I would lose it and find it anew. But I have *always* wanted to be a photographer, ever since my eyes have learned to see rather than just look and ever since I can remember. My first contact with photography was in my earliest childhood.' In fact, Escher took his first pictures with a simple box camera at the age of twelve, developing them himself with the help of a friend.

Escher's parents were not wealthy and at that time photography did not provide a secure means of support. So, at the age of fourteen, he was apprenticed to a locksmith. Following two years of hard physical work, he used his drawing skills to get employment as a technical draftsman at the Ganz ship-building and machinery works. This opened the way to serious photography with a 'real' camera: an Ernemann with an f6.8 anastigmatic lens. A young engineer friend, an amateur photographer, gave him several lessons. 'From then on, I spent all my free time taking and developing pictures and studying the literature. Every Sunday we went on picture-taking excursions, discussing new trends, subjects, the light, framing, and such things', Escher wrote. He was able to make enough money from his next job, as a technician in the Nicholsson machine factory, to buy modern photographic equipment. A group of young amateurs gathered around him, and it was now Escher who was the teacher: 'This collective amateurism proved very useful; everyone in this little group was able to contribute something new, experimenting with, inventing or reading about new things . . . All of us could expand our scope and knowledge . . . all had higher goals and reached for unique artistic heights.'

In 1916, Escher's career took a new turn. Having made a name for himself as an accomplished and technically proficient amateur photographer, he went to work in films. Starting as a sports reporter for the Frölich-Fodor film import company, a year later he was already making feature films for the Astra company. During the 1919 Hungarian Soviet Republic, he made documentary newsreels which are today significant historical documents of the revolution. In the 1920s, he was a feature film cameraman again, working with a number of outstanding artists. The arrival of sound films stopped Hungarian film production for several years. Escher again changed careers: 'In 1928, at thirty-eight years of age, and after a great many detours, I finally reached the goal which, consciously or not, I had always sought, the profession which was my calling: photojournalism.'

For the next three decades, he was the most sought-after photojournalist in Hungary. Rudolph Balogh, outstanding artist-photographer and photojournalist for the newspaper *Pesti Napló* ('Pest Diary'), discovered Escher's talents as a reporter and helped him to get a job with the progressive newspaper *Est* ('Evening') and the illustrated supplement of *Pesti Napló*. After these papers ceased publication, Escher worked for the journals *Hid* ('The Bridge'), *Film-Szinház-Irodalom* ('Film-Theatre-Literature'), and *Szinházi Élet* ('Theatre Life'). Other magazines also published his work and almost every important journal of the time carried his photographs. Equally skilled in photographing political, social and cultural events, he took his camera into Parliament, the slums, theatres and sports fields taking genre pictures, artistic portraits, fashion photographs and masterful animal shots. With unlimited endurance, he could work in the field all day, never requiring editorial guidance; following his reporter's instincts, he was to be found wherever there was an exciting event. After 1945, he worked for the magazines *Képes Világ* ('The World in Pictures'), *Kis Ujság* ('Little paper'), and *Képes Figyelö* ('Pictorial Observer'). Finally, in the years before his retirement, he was on the staff of the *Hungarian Foreign Trade* journal.

Escher's best pictures were also exhibited in photographic exhibitions at home and abroad, and he very soon became renowned for his innovative style. In 1931, he won First Prize in the London Modern Photography exhibition. In 1934 he received the Grand Prix at Milan's World Exhibition of Applied Arts and four years later was awarded the Silver Medal at the Venice Biennale. In 1959, he received the Gold Medal at the Third International Photographic Art Exhibition in Budapest, as well as recognition by the International Federation of Photographic Art (FIAP). In Hungary, he was awarded the Silver Medal of the Order of Labour in 1964, and the title 'Honoured Artist of the Hungarian People's Republic' in 1965. In that year, the Hungarian National Gallery staged his first one-man show, a retrospective of works taken over more than half a century. Its success was the final great reward of his life and he died in Budapest on February 26 1966. Later that year, the first Hungarian exhibition of photographic history, *125 Years of Hungarian Photographic Art,* brought a still wider recognition to Károly Escher's work. In 1966 the first volume of the series *Fotomüvészeti Kiskönyvtár* ('Hungarian Photographers') was called *Foto Escher* and contained 64 of his photographs. The introduction was by a former editor of his, Ernö Mihályfi.

Escher considered the most essential qualifications for a photographer to be broad general education and experience: 'I don't mean professional expertise, that's a natural requisite. Reporting is a field which requires very diverse knowledge. A good photojournalist has to know just about everything.' He himself was not only a master of operating a camera, but a good writer. His book *Photographic Journalism*, and the commemorative text in his photo-album devoted to the great Hungarian actress, Gizi Bajor, are a pleasure to read. And his experience in technical science and chemistry enabled him to successfully solve a problem quite removed from photojournalism: in 1957, he saved a unique national treasure for posterity by chemically restoring the only accredited daguerreotype of the famous poet, Sandor Petofi, which had by that time become almost unrecognizable.

Escher's career as photojournalist began in the very restricted atmosphere of the 1920s. The period between the two World Wars did not give the same broad scope to a realistic, critically outspoken reporter as the previous two decades. A reporter's task was considered to be mere documentation, and magazines published mostly dry, factual, naturalistic pictures, either to accompany a text or to provide a folkloric idyll of peasant life. It is not surprising that the best of the Hungarian reporters, like János Müllner or Gyula Jelfy, were not published by the Hungarian press after 1919. Others, like Andor (André) Kertész, Márton (Martin) Munkácsi or László (Lucien) Aigner, went to work abroad, and thus became famous all over the world. For a while, they kept contact with the press at home and their reports from various parts of the world appeared in Hungarian journals.

Károly Escher remained in Hungary, perfecting his original style. As a good chronicler, he was primarily concerned with being honest, an attitude which determined his whole approach, and even his technique. He refused to use magnesium or flash light, since he felt that only natural light was faithful. Thus he used available light and a high-powered 35mm camera (Leica or, later, Contax), trying to remain a hidden, anonymous observer. This is the secret of the attractively direct truth-to-life of his pictures. His approach was simple and unaffectedly photographic, showing an excellent sense of proportion. He did not strive to be naturalistic, though naturalism is an almost inherent component of photography, and he avoided unusual or distorted perspectives, and other such mannerisms. The message in his pictures is nearly always that of the 'truth'. Escher was able to see how a given subject could best be presented, and what was its inherent form. His composition testifies to an unusually sensitive creative talent. Open to anything, he was a great observer who avoided artificiality, never intervening, but allowing his subject to move freely according to its own laws. He was able to catch just that moment when his subject presented its most natural self.

Escher considered it essential for photojournalism to capture motion. He did not want to stop time and freeze the moment, but to depict action in motion. Even back in the 1930s, when sharp outlines were considered essential to photography, he was ahead of his time in expressing motion through serial-motion photography and using the contrast between sharp and unsharp focus to bring out significant movement. He used this technique particularly in theatre pictures, the most remarkable being those of Béla Bartók's ballet *The Miraculous Mandarin* (page 33, top right). With movements thus intensified, he was able to express great inner tension, rendering a perfect visual image of passions condensed in dynamically powerful music.

As can be seen from his ever-new choice of subjects, Escher kept pace with the rapidly moving events of his time. Change, however, never induced him to photograph the ephemeral. Rather, he captured the essential features of a subject, thereby also uncovering those underlying characteristics which only the artist's eye sees. His photographs have become authentic records of the time. As a devoted press reporter, he could see deeper than those contemporaries who merely sought to document. And what he saw he was able to capture with a unique feeling for the most expressive, the dramatic moment. Escher, who for decades had been present at every significant event in Hungary, wrote history with his camera. From his pictures we can reconstruct the essentials of life between the two World Wars, not through formal events, but through such differing facets of reality as life in the slums, barefooted village children, leaders of intellectual and artistic life.

As with all great artists who deal with problems of general interest, the focus of Escher's art was man. He was not politically inclined, and he did not participate in any political movement, but his pictures are unintentionally political. His instinctive bourgeois radicalism, his humanistic outlook and passionate sense of justice led him not only to capture the facts but to express an opinion, adding his own personality to the subject of his works. He had compassion for those who suffered, and stood alongside those who spoke out against injustice, sometimes using satire to do so.

Escher's ability to condense the social problems of the time, with its hopelessness and bitterness, is well expressed in *The Blind Musician* (page 34). Even more unsettling is his series *The Evicted*, with its depressing impotent helplessness and weary indifference. Escher achieves such emotional effects not through sentimentalism or shocking naturalistic details. His simple journalistic statements underline artistically through forceful symbolism something socially universal, shedding light on man's inhumanity to man. Each photograph in the series depicts a typical figure and his fate at the time of Hungary's great economic crisis.

At times Escher could express the universally valid through quite close examination of his subject. In *Destitute*, we see only a pair of feet in torn shoes; in *Slumhouse in the Outskirts* (page 36 bottom) we see the inhumane living conditions in the dark corner of a hut, two children left near the iron stove. *Night Refuge* is a photograph of crowded, yet lonely, weary and withdrawn figures, the composition expressing the subject's hopelessness. In *Construction Labourers* (page 37 top), on the other hand, the workers walking diagonally across the picture give a sense of the strength and energy of working together.

In his genre pictures of peasants, too, Escher – contrary to official cultural policy – noted the realities of village life, in contrast to its picturesque depiction by amateur photographers. In the words of Ernö Mihályfi: 'He reported like those sociologists studying village life who see beyond the colourful folkloric costumes to the consumption-stricken humans underneath.' *Resting Harvesters* reveals just how exhaustive and hard the work of these people is.

Escher's ability to see beyond the surface of things was evident in other aspects of his life. With sympathy and a sense of humour, he discovered the hidden comic features in a face, a gesture or a situation. But he always remained on the joyfully humorous level of the little man; as soon as his subject was from a higher social stratum, his compassionate smile disappeared, his tone became ironic and satirical. His *Bank Manager at the Public Baths* (page 28) shows a conceited figure floating on the water like a ridiculously blown-up balloon, its grotesqueness increased by the distorted view-point. His picture *Wait and See* (below) shows his lack of interest in ceremony, pompous parades or illustrious participants; rather, he photographs the unfortunate sweeper, ready to leap into action behind a row of mounted policemen. The parallel with his great French contemporary Henri Cartier-Bresson is clear.

Sometimes, Escher made an every-day topic into something more, showing an additional potent symbol, even independently of the actual subject. *The Horse of the Apocalypse* (page 35) was made at an agricultural exhibition. But the rumbling dark mass of the huge galloping stallion and the foreboding dark clouds, are a frightening symbol of approaching war. On the war itself Escher commented through a startling pair of pictures of two pairs of eyes. Those impertinently self-confident belong to a flower-crowned *Soldier Off to War* (page 38); those shell-shocked are a *Homecoming Soldier* (page 39), who has been through hell.

Escher captured events through movement and change. His portraits, too, are journalistic. He never took his subjects – writers, artists or scientists – into a studio, but caught them in their natural surroundings, in characteristic moments, experiencing inner or outer events which testify to their character or creative work, their artistic or intellectual world. Often these are playfully humorous: 'My editor told me that I musn't bring him some stereotype photo of Piccard', Escher said of this picture (opposite). 'When I told the professor this, he started making faces: 'Is this OK?' – and I released the shutter.'

Karoly Escher's pictures need no commentary, or explanatory text. They speak for themselves, because the artist thought through pictures. So it is not surprising that most of them appeared in picture supplements of magazines with only a line or two of accompanying text. Among the photojournalists who stayed in Hungary, he was almost alone in following his profession on such a high level. And he created and found the most appropriate, modern, apparently artless form for his message. His formal composition never appeared for its own end and to the detriment of the content, but rather as subordinate to it, increasing the force of what he wanted to say.

Klára Tóry
(Translated by Krisztina Rozsnyai)

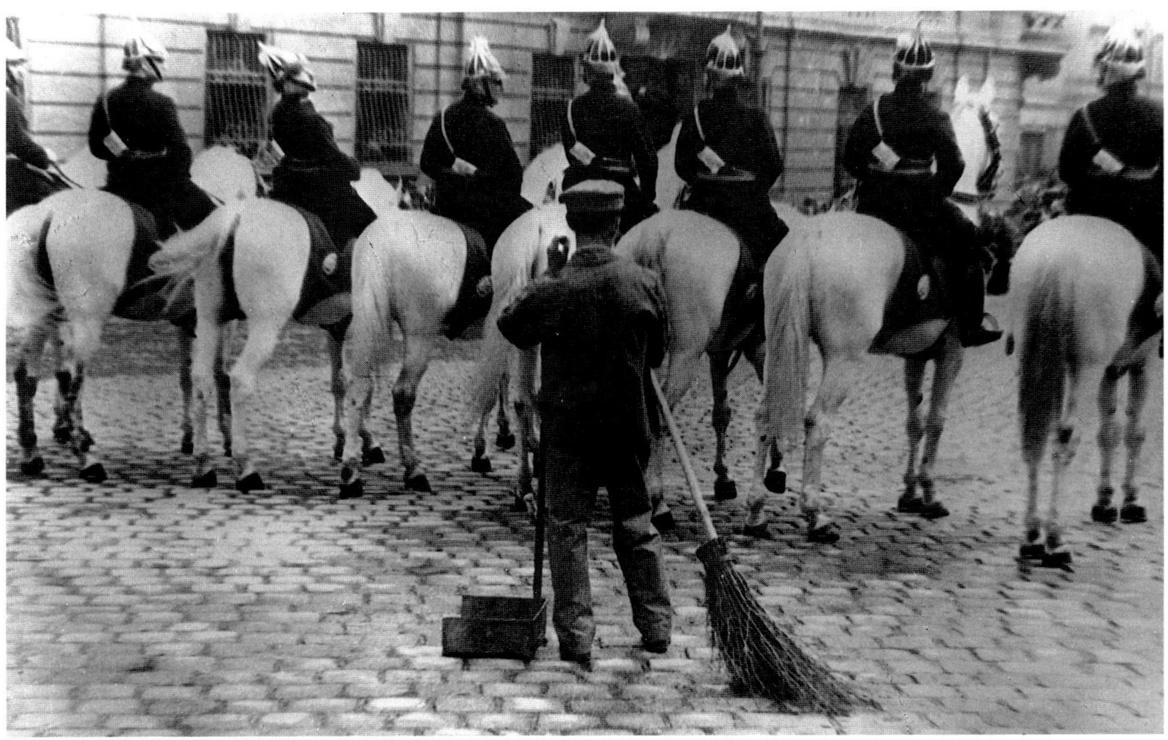

Károly Escher: *Wait and See,* 1934

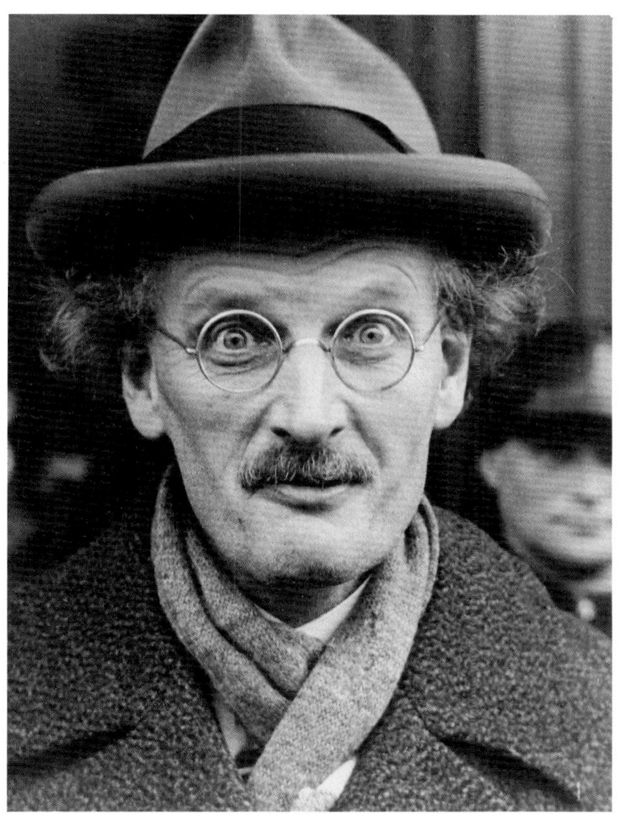

Károly Escher: *Professor Piccard*, 1930s

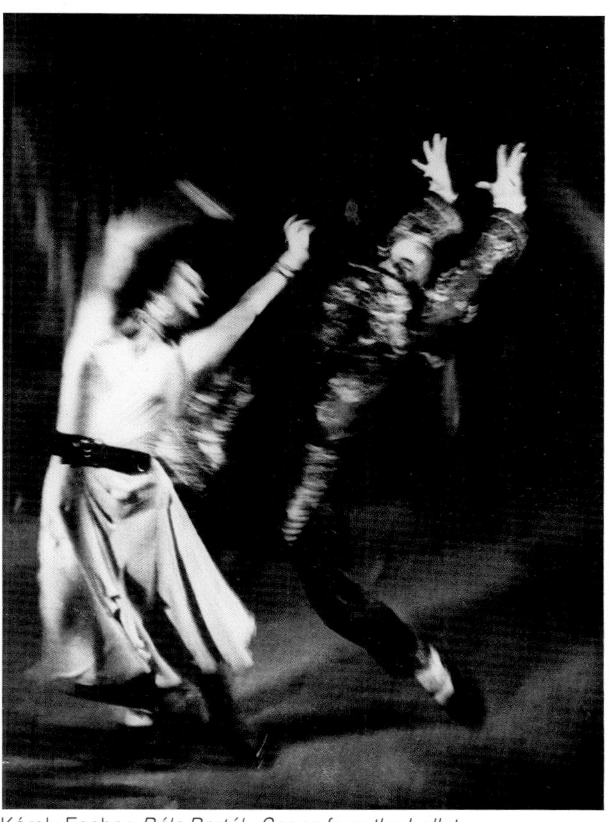

Károly Escher: *Béla Bartók: Scene from the ballet 'The Miraculous Mandarin'*, 1956

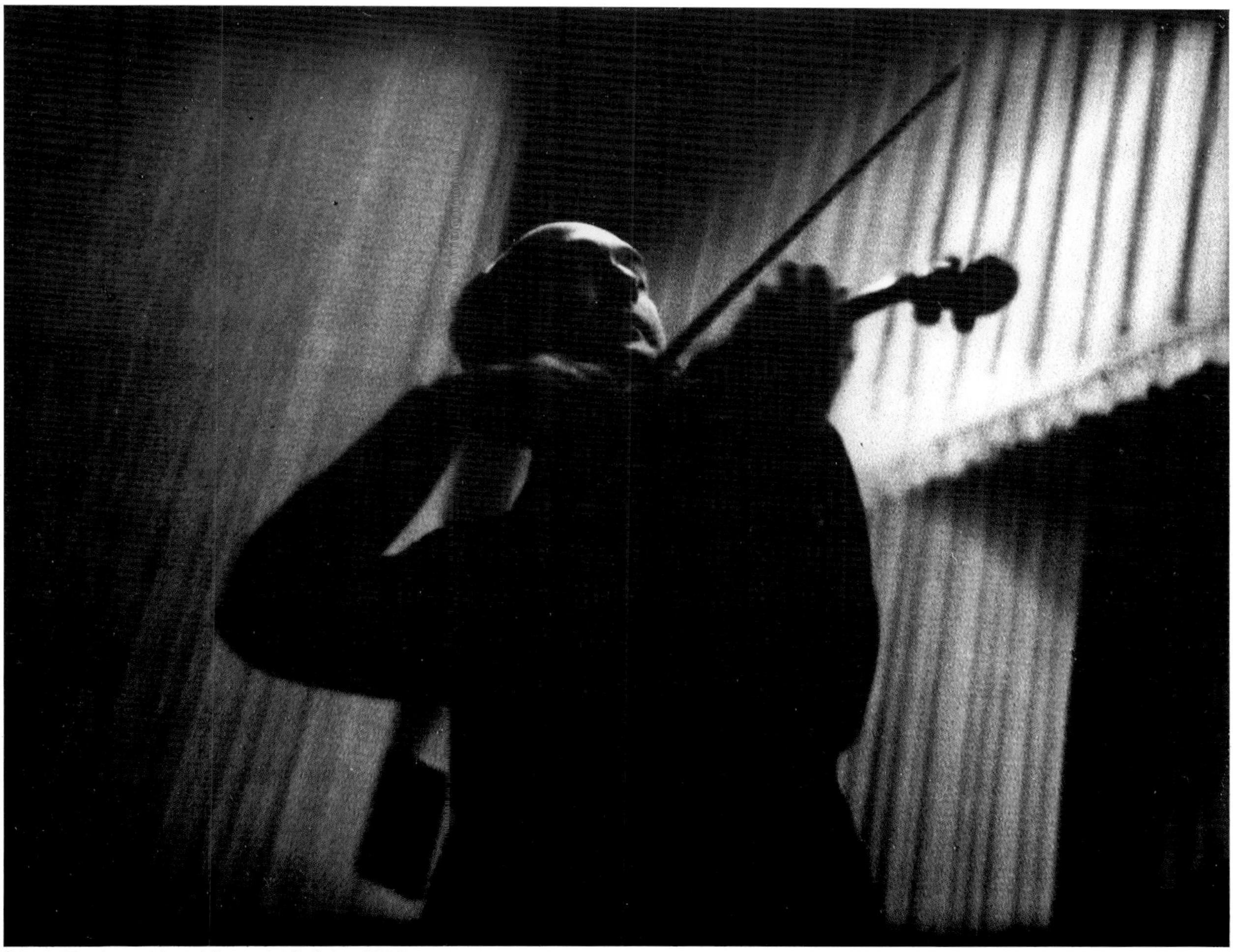

Károly Escher: *József Szigeti, Violinist*, 1933

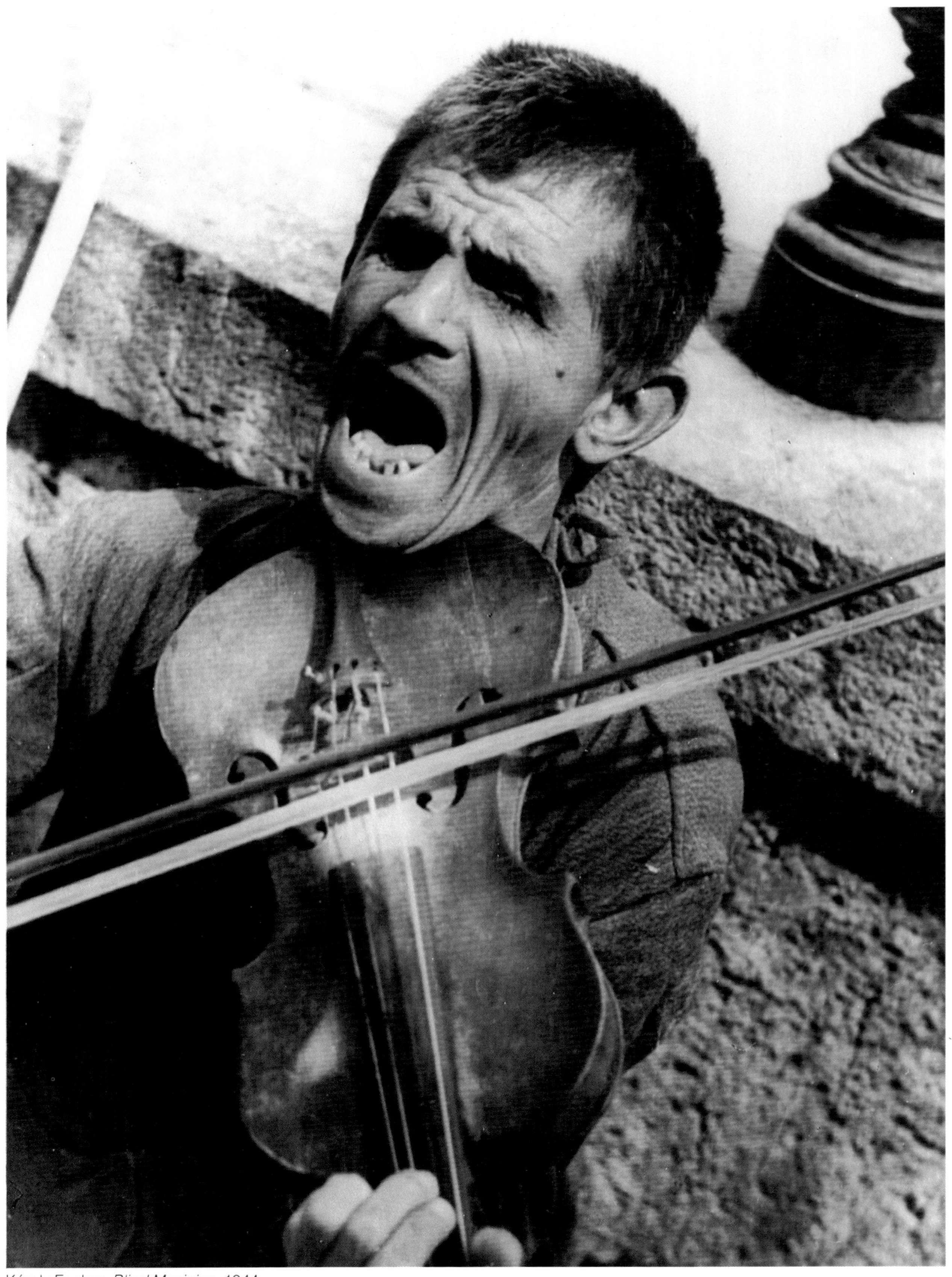

Károly Escher: *Blind Musician,* 1944

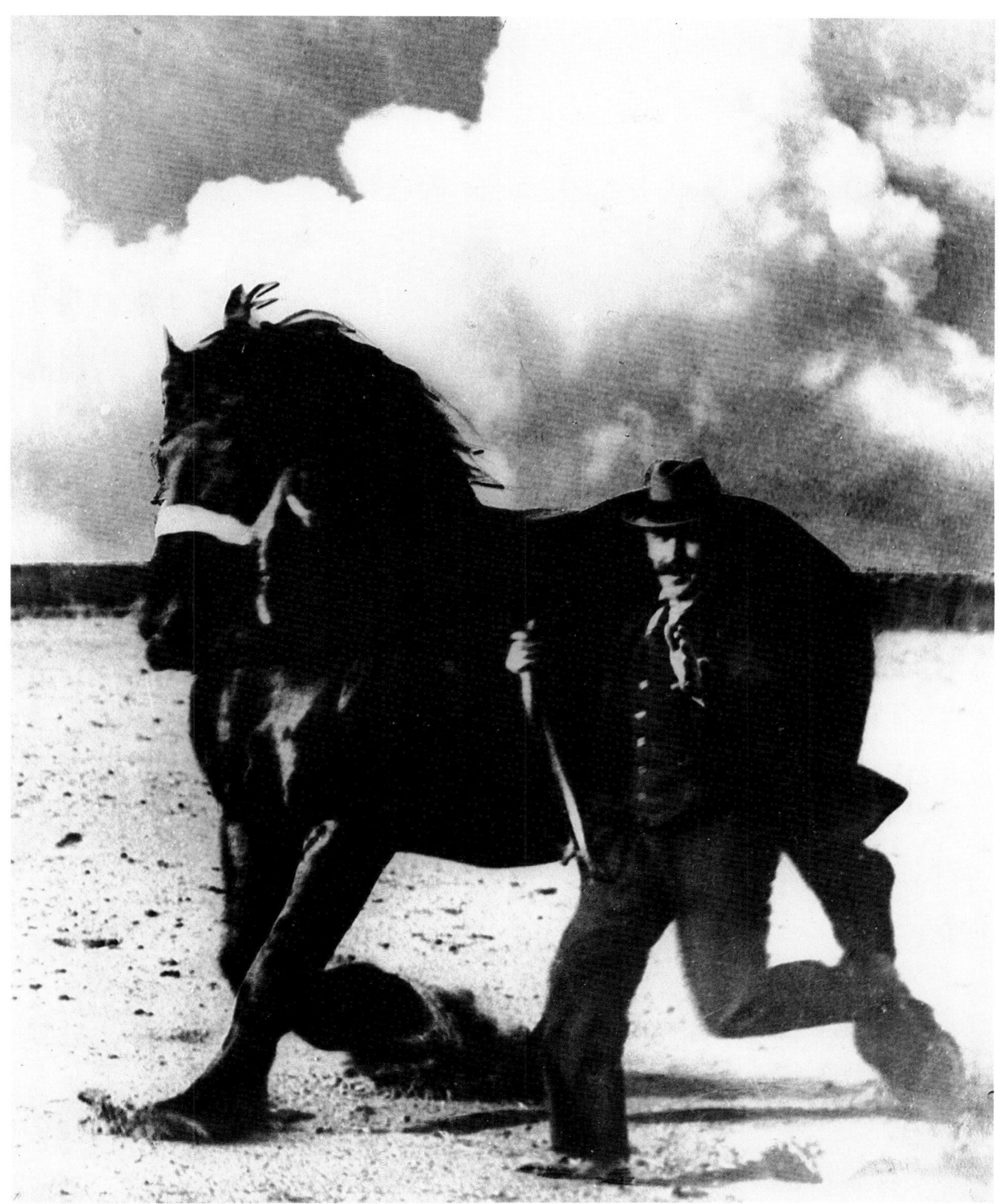

Károly Escher: *The Horse of the Apocalypse,* 1937

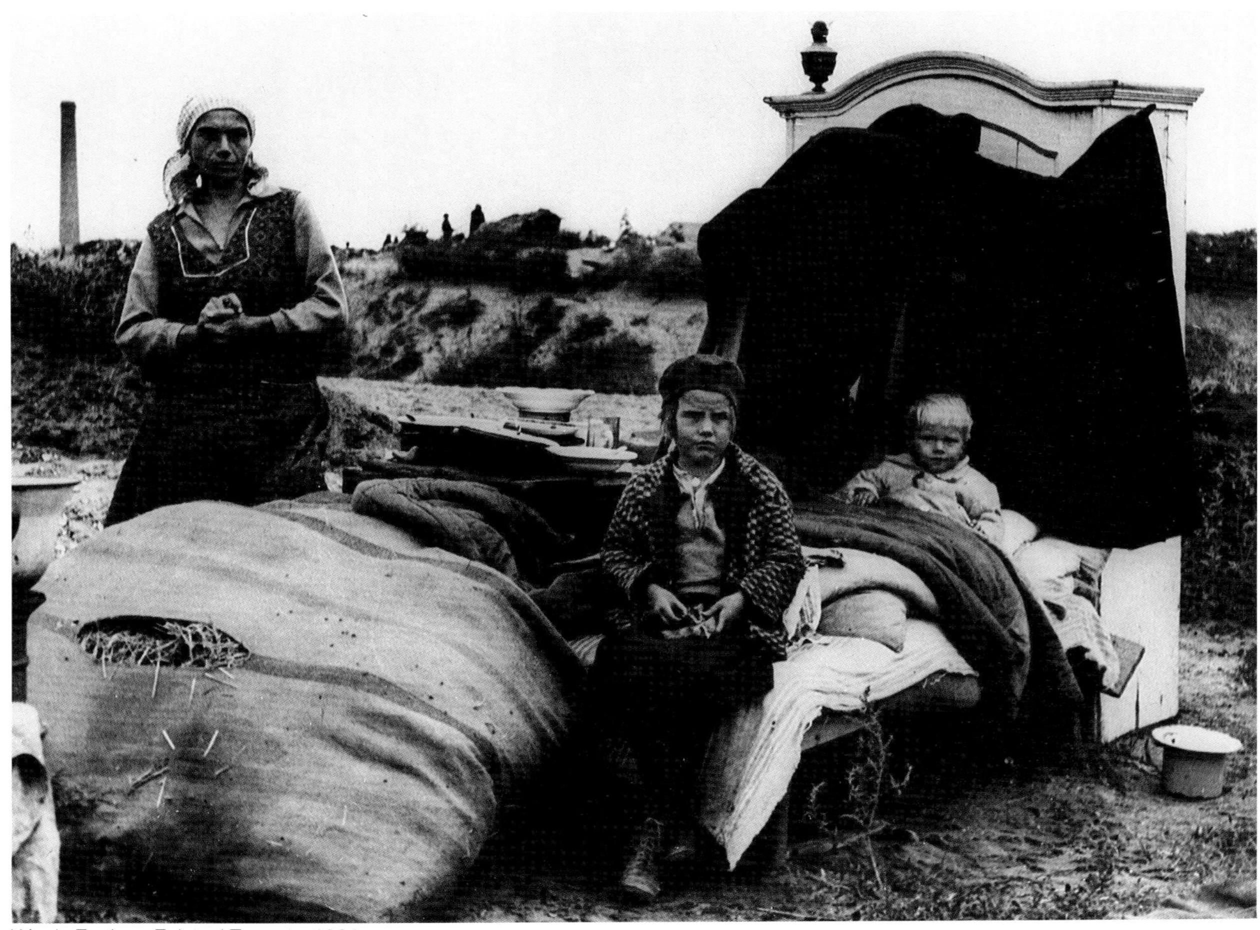

Károly Escher: *Evicted Tenants,* 1934

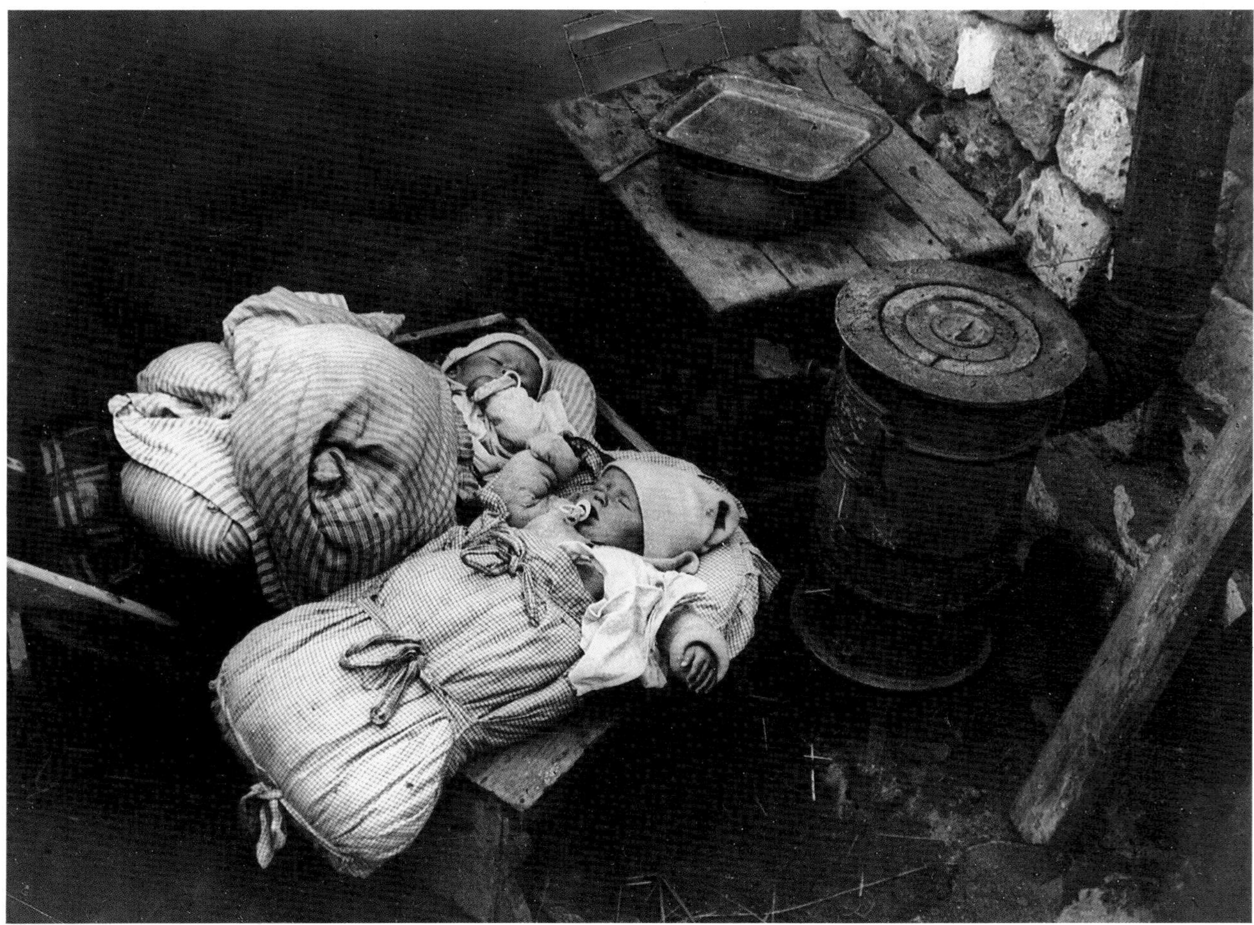

Károly Escher: *Slumhouse in the Suburb,* 1932

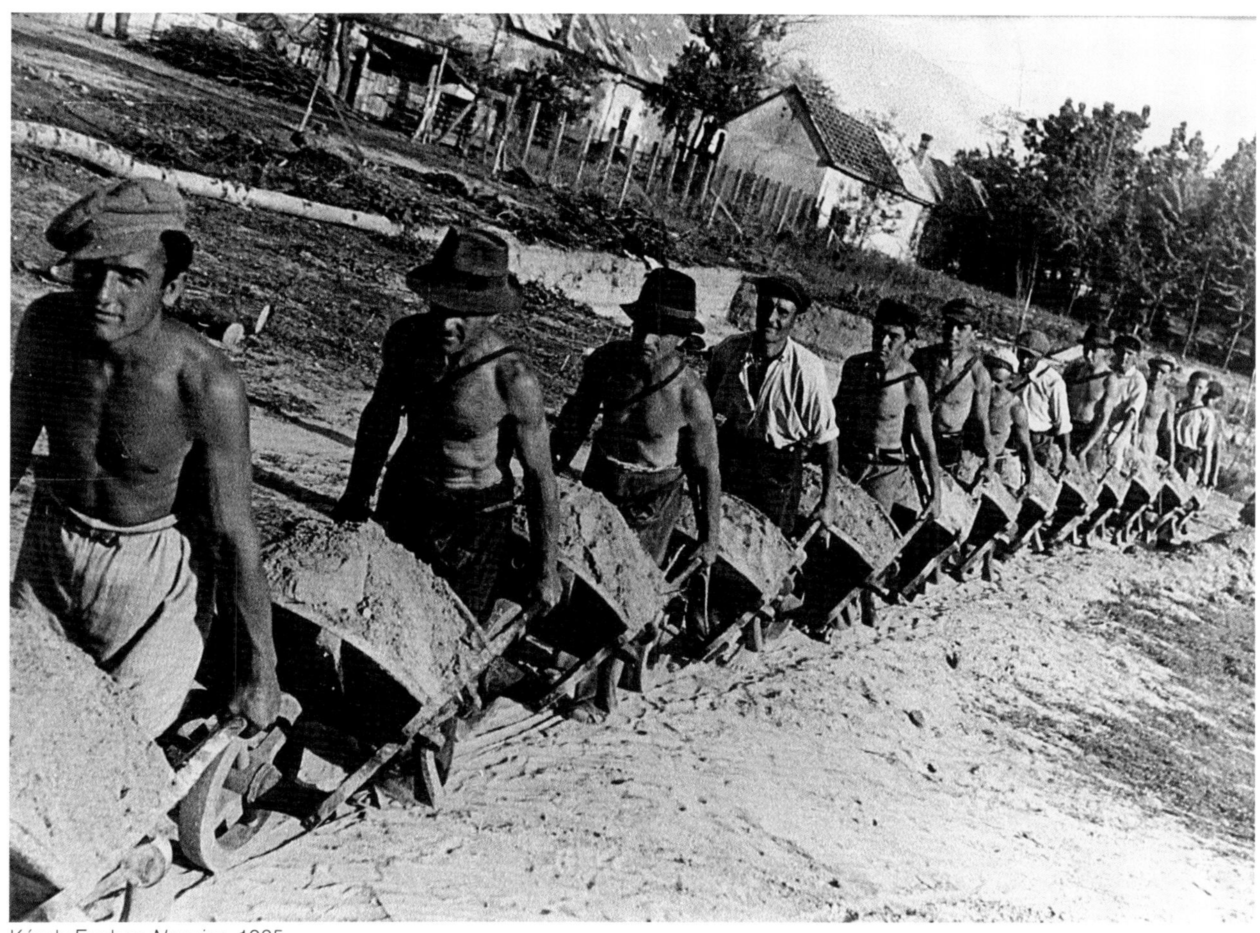

Károly Escher: *Navvies*, 1935

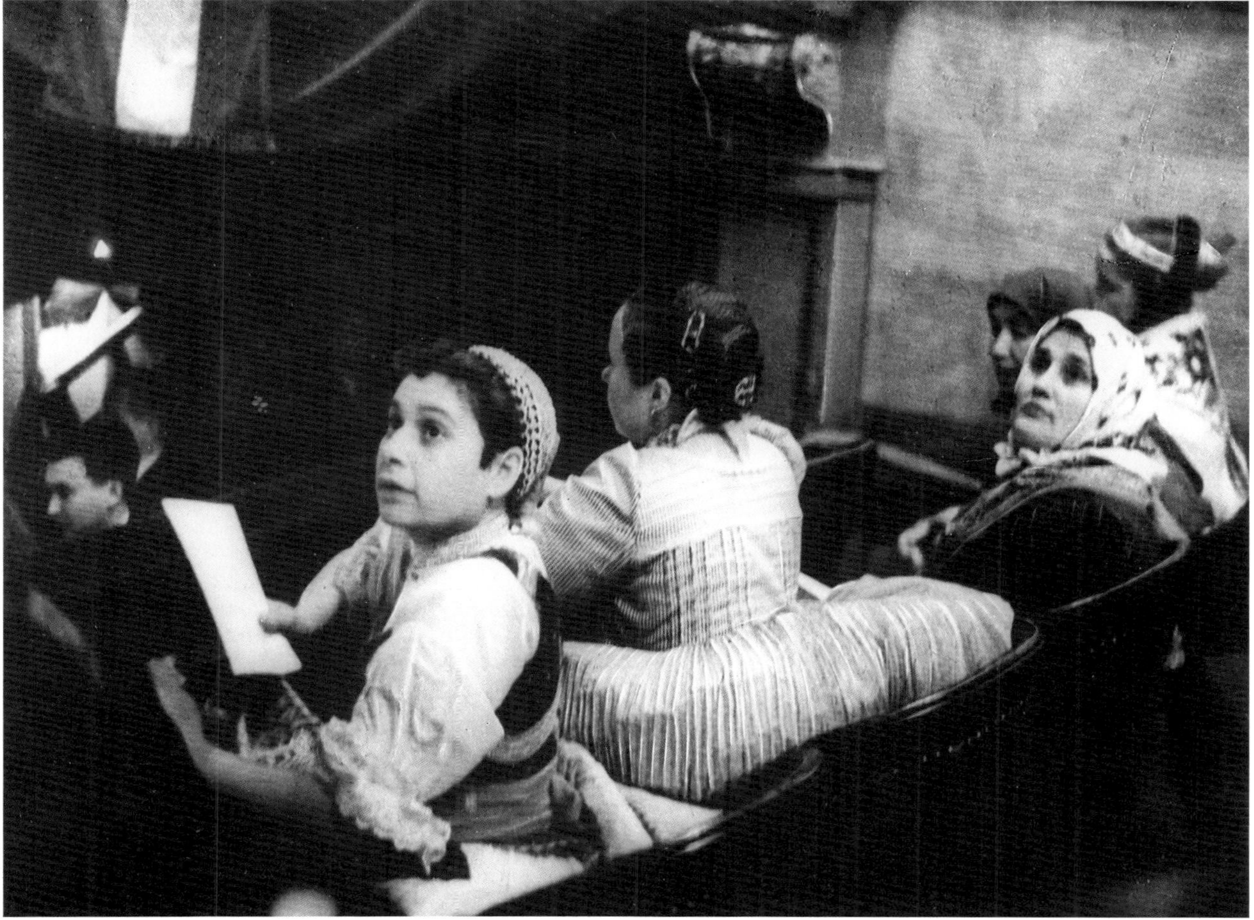

Károly Escher: *New Audience in the Opera-house*, 1948

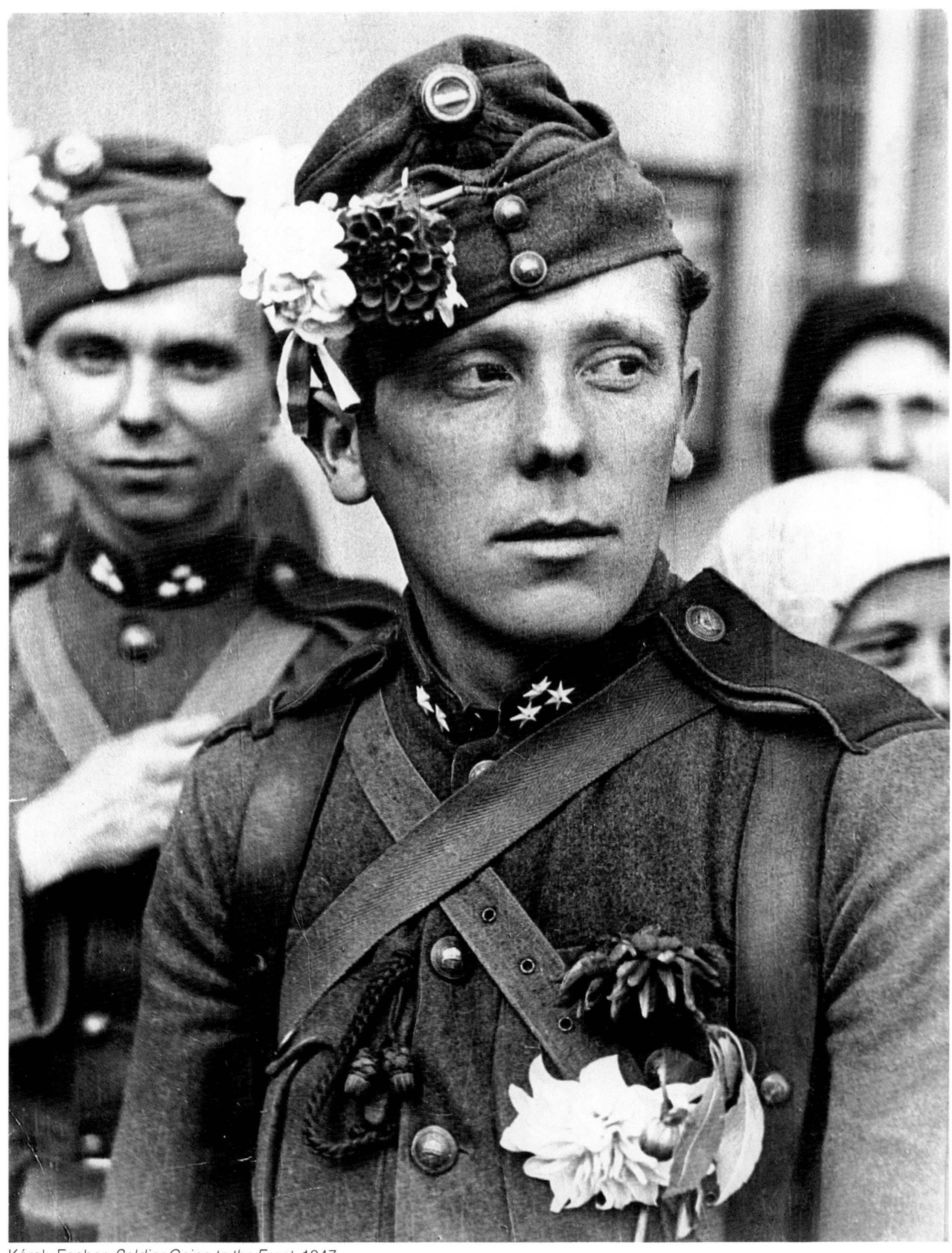
Károly Escher: *Soldier Going to the Front,* 1947

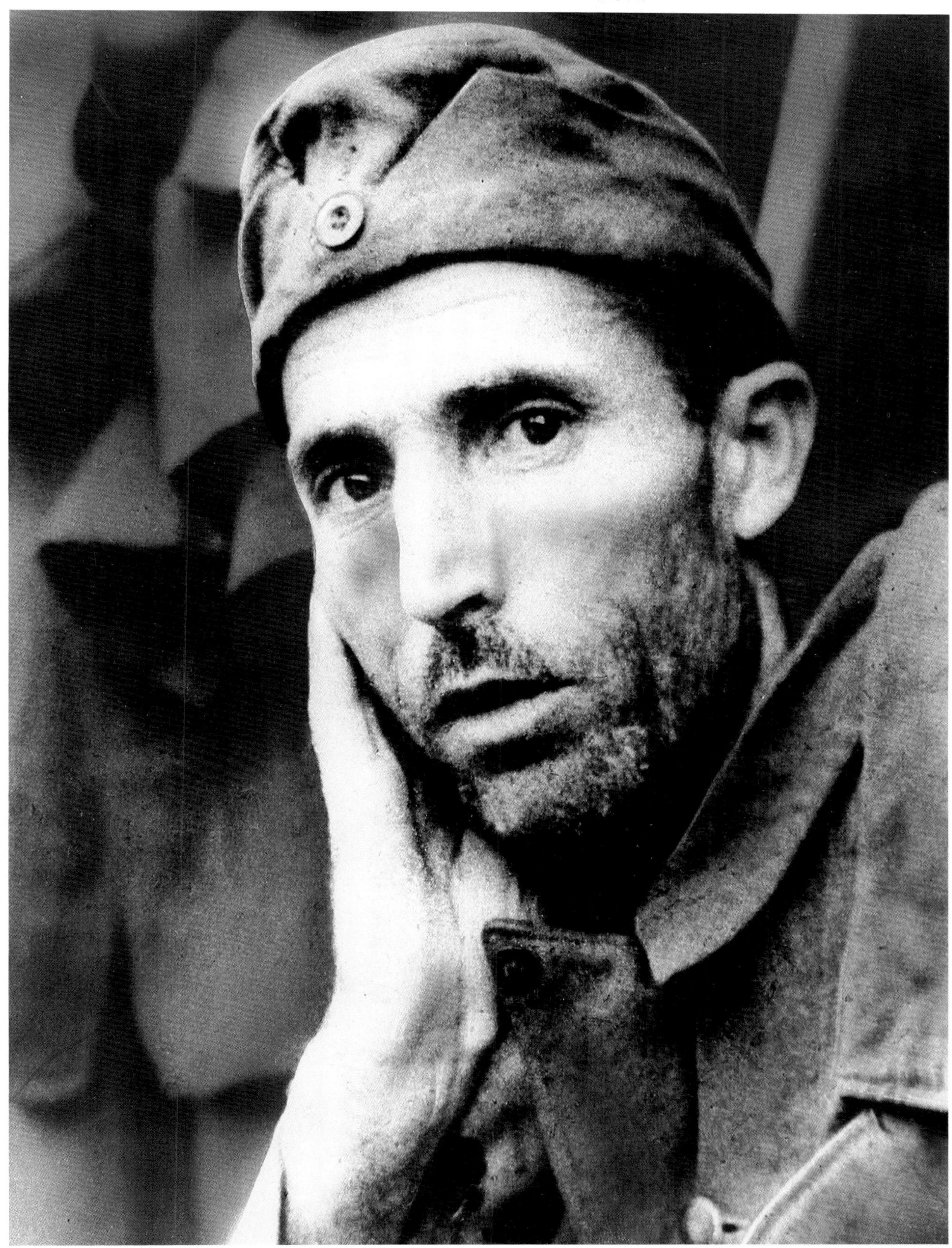

Károly Escher: *Homecoming Soldier*, 1947

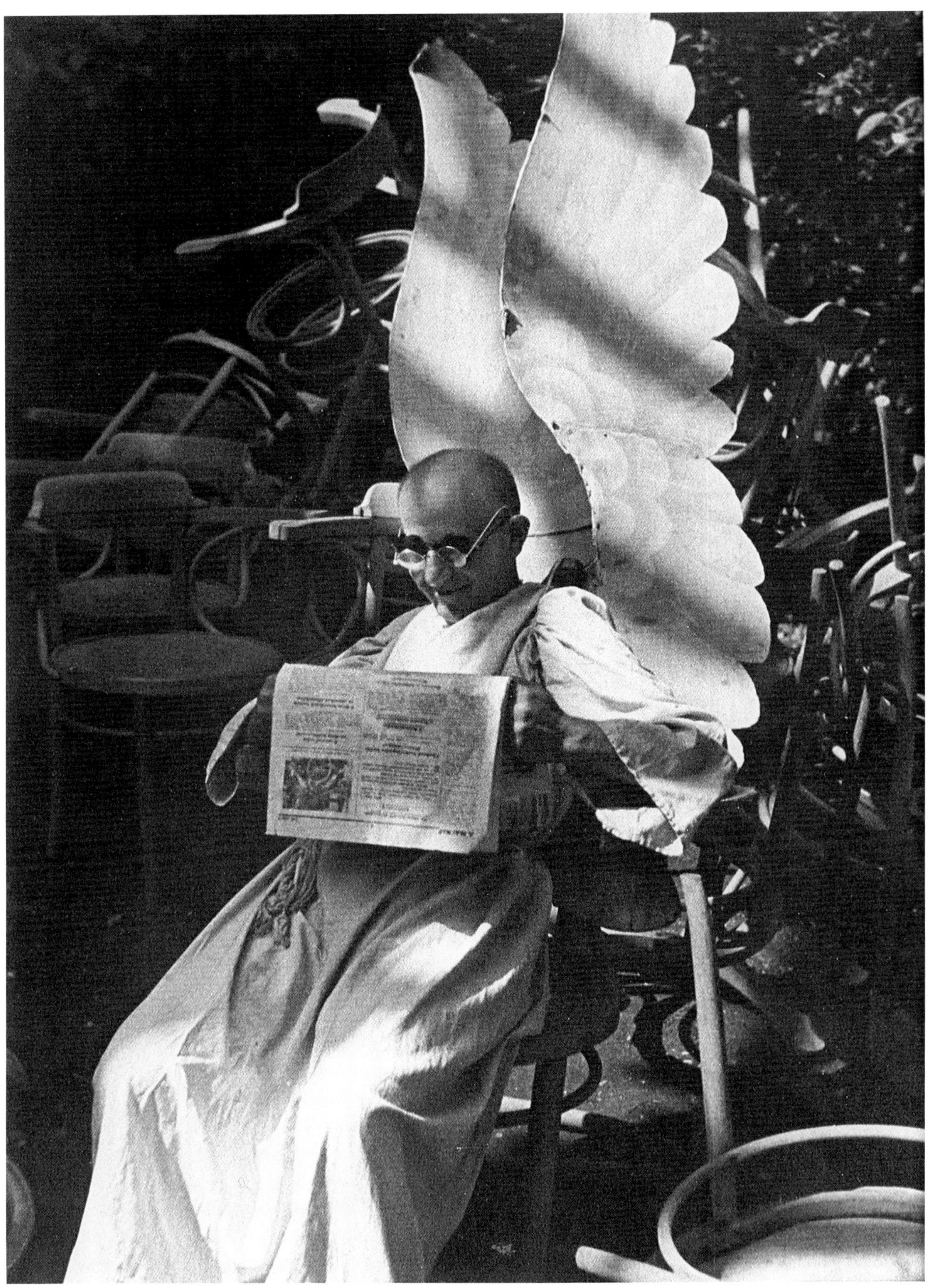

Károly Escher: *Angel of Peace*, 1938